C000199021

On Hunting

Also by Roger Scruton

Philosophy
Art and Imagination
The Aesthetics of Architecture
A Dictionary of Political Thought
Sexual Desire
Modern Philosophy
An Intelligent Person's Guide to Philosophy
The Aesthetics of Music

Essays
The Meaning of Conservatism
Untimely Tracts
The Philosopher on Dover Beach
Fiction
Fortnight's Anger
Francesca
A Dove Descending and other Stories
Xanthippic Dialogues

ON HUNTING

Roger Scruton

YELLOW JERSEY PRESS
LONDON

Published by Yellow Jersey Press 1998

2 4 6 8 10 9 7 5 3 1

First published in Great Britain in 1998 by
Yellow Jersey Press
Random House, 20 Vauxhall Bridge Road,
London SW1V 2SA

Random House Australia (Pty) Limited
20 Alfred Street, Milsons Point, Sydney,
New South Wales 2061, Australia

Random House New Zealand Limited
18 Poland Road, Glenfield,
Auckland 10, New Zealand

Random House South Africa (Pty) Limited
Endulini, 5A Jubilee Road, Parktown 2193, South Africa

Random House UK Limited Reg. No. 954009

A CIP catalogue record for this book
is available from the British Library

ISBN 0 224 05153 9

Papers used by Random House UK Limited are natural,
recyclable products made from wood grown in sustainable
forests. The manufacturing processes conform to the
environmental regulations of the country of origin.

Typeset by Deltatype Ltd, Birkenhead, Merseyside
Printed and bound in Great Britain by
Butler and Tanner Ltd, Frome and London

To Christina Stranescu, and the future of hunting.

What do the dead do, Uncle? Do they eat,
Hear music, go a-hunting, and be merry
As we that live?

Webster, *The White Devil*

Contents

Preface   xi

Prologue   1

Chapter One: Apologia pro Vita Sua   7

Chapter Two: Beginning   38

Chapter Three: Intermezzo – The Philosophy of
   Hunting   62

Chapter Four: Middle   80

Chapter Five: End?   128

Epilogue   155

Preface

Hunting with hounds is a craft requiring both stamina and skill. It was already well established in antiquity, and Xenophon's treatise on the subject shows how similar were the techniques used by huntsmen in ancient Greece to those used today. Similar too were the attitudes – towards hounds, towards followers of the hunt, and towards the countryside. Dissimilar, however, was the quarry. Xenophon pursued hares, deer and wild boar, the first for sport, the second and third in order to gain full control of the land needed for agriculture.

Fox-hunting as we know it is largely an English invention. It began during the seventeenth century as an aristocratic pursuit, made attractive by the dwindling supply of wild deer; it was made into a science by Hugo Meynell (1727–1808), founder of the Quorn foxhounds in Leicestershire; and fox-hunts were schools for the cavalry during the Napoleonic wars. Throughout this time foxes were regarded as vermin; they were neither protected by the Game Laws, nor reserved for the amusement of the gentry. Anybody was entitled to kill them. Hence those who would kill foxes in other ways than by hunting them, such as farmers and labourers, acquired a new social impor-

tance. They had to be persuaded to conserve the
pests which threatened their livelihood.

One way of doing this was to permit the rural work-
force to join in the fun. Gradually the fox-hunt became
the melting pot of country society. 'It links all classes
together,' wrote John Hawkes in 1808, 'from the Peer
to the Peasant. It is the Englishman's peculiar privilege. It is not to be found in any other part of the globe,
but in England's true land of liberty.' Many people
responded to hunting in that way: it seemed both to
perpetuate the class system, and also to soften it.
Liberty, the mark of aristocracy, was now bestowed on
all – and the living proof of this was hunting.

The history of this curious sport, and its astonishing
impact on the social and physical development of our
country, has been told several times, most recently by
Sir Raymond Carr (*English Foxhunting*, Oxford 1976),
David C. Itzkowitz (*Peculiar Privilege: A Social History
of English Foxhunting*, Harvester Press 1977) and Jane
Ridley (*Fox Hunting*, Collins 1990). The technique too
has been the subject of countless tracts and manuals, of
which the best are Peter Beckford's *Thoughts on
Hunting*, which first appeared in 1781, and *The Diary of
a Huntsman*, published in 1836 and written by Thomas
Smith.

This book, however, is neither a manual, nor a
history, nor a justification of fox-hunting, but simply
an account of one man's involvement in it. It is an
involvement which changed my life.

Malmesbury, February 1998

Prologue

'Of all things in this world, Fox-hunting is the most difficult thing to explain to those who know nothing about it.' The words are those of Lord Willoughby de Broke in an anthology published just after the end of the First World War. The title of the book – *The Sport of our Ancestors* – is as anachronistic as the title of its author. And neither will endear hunting to those who heartily dislike it, and who find their feelings captured by Oscar Wilde's most famous – and weakest – quip. 'The unspeakable in full pursuit of the uneatable' is false at both ends. Most of those who hunt are ordinary decent people who stand, in my experience, noticeably above the moral norm. And the fox is uneatable only to fastidious aesthetes like Wilde.*

Hunting, like shooting and fishing, is a sport, though one with many strange and festive qualities,

---

* After skinning and cleaning the fox, you should marinate it for a day in brine, so as to remove the pungent aroma; then wash it in running water for five minutes, joint it as you would a hare, marinate again for six hours in red wine, with onion, garlic and herbs, etc., and proceed as you would for jugged hare. Capers, green peppercorns, diced bacon, mushrooms and juniper berries are all welcome additions.

some of which I try to explain in this book. For many
people, sport is the nub of their life and the focus of
their leisure. This fact is so familiar to us that we
scarcely wonder at it. Yet it needs an explanation –
particularly when we recall that the most popular
sports are those, like football, whose followers take
no apparent part in the game. What is it that
motivates the football fan – what generates that blind
addiction to his team and identification with its
fortunes, which threaten to displace all other waking
concerns from his affections? What is it that leads
him to sally forth each Saturday, to cheer and shout
at an event which has no perceivable purpose besides
the shunting of a ball around a lozenge of grass, and
which, when completed, leaves the world exactly as it
was when the game began? Why is it that people
ignorant of their national heroes, of their monarchs,
statesmen, poets and scientists, will nevertheless
rattle off the names of the Arsenal eleven and supply
each with an adoring biography?

Look back to the first flowering of our civilisation
in ancient Greece, and you will find sport already in
the centre of social life, a focus of loyalties, a rehearsal
of military prowess and a pious tribute to the gods.
Pindar wrote in praise of winners at the pan-Hellenic
games. But his odes are not records of fleeting
victories. They are descriptions of the gods and their
stories, invocations of the divine presence in a place
and a time, and an exalted celebration of what it
means to be a Hellene among Hellenes, sharing
language, history, divinities and fate. They show us

the spectator as another participant. His excited cheers, we recognize, are brought up from the very depths of his social being, as a contribution to the action and a kind of recreation of the religious sense.

So it is with modern football. The spectator is also a participant, contributing precisely through the loyalty that glues his eyes to the pitch.

One thing I know for sure about being a fan is this: it is not a vicarious pleasure, despite all appearances to the contrary, and those who say they would rather do than watch are missing the point. Football is a context where watching *becomes* doing ... when there is some kind of triumph, the pleasure does not radiate from the players outwards until it reaches the likes of us at the back of the terraces in a pale and diminished form; our fun is not a watery version of the team's fun, even though they are the ones that get to score the goals and climb the steps at Wembley to meet Princess Diana. The joy we feel on occasions like this is not a celebration of others' good fortune, but a celebration of our own; and when there is a disastrous defeat the sorrow that engulfs us is, in effect, self-pity, and anyone who wishes to understand how football is consumed must realise this above all things. The players are merely our representatives, chosen by the manager rather than elected by us, but our representatives none-theless, and sometimes if you look hard enough you can see the little poles that join them together,

and the handles at the side that enable us to move
them. I am a part of the club, just as the club is a
part of me...*

Nick Hornby vividly describes the sense of membership that ties the fan to the team, and makes every
cheer and groan into an act of participation. But why
should this experience be so all-engrossing and
obsessive? What in our nature requires it, and why is
it so widely observed? Those are the questions which
this book sets out to answer.

Among the many misconceptions surrounding
hunting, none is more common than the belief that
those who hunt, unlike those who attend a football
match, are part of the action. On the contrary,
hunting is as much, and as little, a spectator sport as
football. True, you can watch what is happening only
if you strive to keep up with the hounds – something
that you can do successfully on horseback but not as
a rule in a car or on foot. Hence each hunt has a field
of followers, stampeding after the pack with every
appearance of being as much concerned in the
business as the hounds themselves. With a few
exceptions these enthusiasts are no more part of the
action than those who follow by car or bicycle on the
roads, or those who run on foot in the wake of the
horses, hoping for a glimpse of the chase. Hunting, as
practised in Britain, is a sport of followers. And its

* Nick Hornby, *Fever Pitch*, London 1996 (Indigo Edition), pp.
186–7.

mystery and emotional power stem in part from the fact that the 'team' you follow, and whose triumphs and disasters you share, is not a group of human beings but a pack of foxhounds.

CHAPTER ONE

Apologia pro Vita Sua

My life divides into three parts. In the first I was wretched; in the second ill at ease; in the third hunting. Most hunting people are brought up in the sport, and shaped by it into a kind of intermediate species, an ancient synthesis of horse, hound and human. Even now I have the sense of hovering on the periphery of the rite, a fascinated spectator of something which has come into being like a language, to be passed down the generations and absorbed from birth, and which can be learned in later life only at the cost of speaking with a foreign accent.

My distance from the heart of things does not detract from the sport. On the contrary, it enhances it. Looking on this intense and natural society, moving with it and sharing its moods, I become reconciled to my own position as an observer. Once it was I who contained the world — a private, bookish world, improvised from ruined dreams. I was the existentialist hero of a drama scripted by myself. I contain the world no longer — I am contained by it. And it is a public, objective, concrete world, whose

rules were established without my help and with no
knowledge of my existence. I have lost my pride, and
gained my composure.

Before summarizing this cautionary tale, however,
a note on autobiographies. The length of a biography
ought to be dictated by the greatness of the deeds
recorded in it. Thousand-page accounts of minor
politicians are the greatest offence against literature –
especially when written by the politicians themselves.
Worst of all are those instant hagiographies of pop
stars, business moguls and dead princesses – works
which pruriently research each detail, and which, by
being true to the facts, are false through and through
in sentiment. Were biographers to confine themselves, like Plutarch and Aubrey, to twenty pages a
time, they would understand their victims more
completely. What follows is a short apology for a life
which is of interest to me but not, on the whole, to
you. I include it because it explains what I love about
hunting.

I went to school in High Wycombe, then a small
market town, which had grown prosperous through
the manufacture of kitchen tables and Windsor
chairs. Most of this furniture was made from
beechwood brought down from the ancient woods
that adorned the Chilterns and which have since been
decimated. My father came to the area during the
war, when he was serving with the ground force of
bomber command. Until this time he had known only
the smog of Manchester, the guilt-ridden gloom of a

non-conformist upbringing, the poverty and bitterness of life in the slums. His family home was in Ancoats, among long Victorian terraces which radiated from the red brick cotton mill where his mother had begun work at the age of thirteen. Sixty years on she was still working there. Then one day she was taken poorly, went home without a murmur, and died.

Her husband had been a drunkard, unemployed because unemployable. He had abused his seven children, fighting them with fists and kitchen knives, and locking them away for days should they displease him, which generally they did. This experience marked my father indelibly. So too did the death from TB of his favourite sister. But by far the worst thing that happened to him during his childhood was his father's insistence, which no amount of imploring could overcome, that he leave school at the earliest legal age (fourteen in those days), and work at some menial task that would cure him of his treasonable hopes — for Jack Scruton had indicated, in vague but unmistakable terms, that he aspired towards a better life than the life of Capel Street. After two years collecting horse manure in the street, Jack saved himself by joining the RAF.

My mother was a shy, gentle girl who had lost her father (also from TB) when she was four. My maternal grandmother had social ambitions of a *thé-dansant* kind. These caused her to bestow on my mother names so embarrassing that they did not survive childhood. As soon as she could speak for

herself, Beryl Clarys adopted the nickname 'Johnny'.
Meanwhile she was palmed off on a cousin, whom my
grandmother called 'Nanny' in order to claim some
further social kudos from the deal.

Nanny was a member of the Plymouth Brethren
and allowed neither dolls nor toys nor small talk; but
she was all that my mother knew of love. The family
never came to terms with the fact that my mother,
their only marriageable relative, had thrown herself
away on a Mancunian prole. For them, Jack spelled
the end of vague but tenacious hopes of a peerage, a
knighthood, a country estate or at the very least an
invitation to dinner with the Mayor.

My parents met in High Wycombe during the
war. My father was soon posted North, where I and
my two sisters were born. But our parents had never
forgotten the tranquil Chiltern villages where they
had done their courting, and at the first opportunity
the family moved back to Wycombe, where my father
prepared himself for civilian life by attending a
teacher-training course.

Apart from a short spell in nearby Marlow, we
remained in High Wycombe until my mother died. I
was brought up in the shadow of my father's two
ruling emotions. One was a love of the English
countryside, as a place unique in its history, appearance and meaning. The other was a hatred of the
upper class. For Jack Scruton class war was the
dominant fact of English life, the deep cause of all
other conflicts, and the explanation of his growing
quarrel with my mother. His love and his hatred had

come together in a mythopoeic version of English history. The countryside, according to Jack Scruton, had been created by a Saxon peasantry, grazing their cattle in peace on common land. It had been stolen by Norman war-lords, who bound the English in feudal chains. The church stood side-by-side with the barons, fattening parsons at the people's cost. A yet more ruthless upper class emerged, enclosing the commons and driving the people to the towns, there to fend off death as best they could. Every now and then, however, the English reclaimed their ancient rights, in peasants' revolts, Luddite rebellions, trade union marches and teachers' strikes. No episode of history had more meaning for Jack than the civil war, when, according to his version, the rugged band of roundheads defended their native soil against the corrupt cavaliers who sought to own, exploit and destroy it. John Hampden's refusal to pay ship money had for ever glorified in my father's eyes the village which bore that hero's name. He would have dearly loved to be schoolmaster there, and might even have obtained the job, had he not refused to declare himself a communicant member of the Church of England (it was a Church of England school), explaining to the committee that the C of E was just another part of the ruling conspiracy and that in any case he was an atheist. My father was a man of principle, who found his principles confirmed in the unremitting failure which they brought on him.

His bitterness was greatly increased by the election of a Conservative government in 1951. This convinced him that the ruling class would always get the upper hand, if only by deception. Nor was he soothed by my mother's lingering vision of a more genteel life than the one so far provided. She had made compromises for my father's sake: lunch was called 'dinner' and supper 'tea'; she abstained in his presence from coffee and served tea which was strong, dark and forbidding, drunk from plain blue-striped mugs like the Salvation Army soup which had saved the Scrutons during the lean years of the Depression. The wireless was for news, comment, football, and for Ludwig Koch on bird-song. But never the Archers, never Woman's Hour, never any of the cosy crystallized-violet stuff that reminded her of the life and dreams of the suburbs. And she went along with his educational routine: Enid Blyton and Beatrix Potter were banned, since they polluted the image of the countryside with cosy bourgeois senti-ment and turned our wild Saxon inheritance into a suburban fairy-tale. Toys were frowned upon, and besides we could not afford them. For entertainment he permitted outdoor games, and the Penguin trans-lation of the Odyssey. Television came, because our maternal grandmother made a gift of one; but it was seldom switched on. And we were sent each Sunday to a bleak Baptist chapel, a place so cold and miserable and guilt-ridden that he himself set foot there only once, in order to ascertain that his children would be sufficiently depressed by it.

Despite these privations, Jack suspected my mother of a deep-down complicity with the old ruling

class. Nor was he wrong. When he had left for
school, we discovered, she drank coffee from china
cups, read social bulletins and romantic fiction, was
wafted by the wireless into 'the Palm Court of Grand
Hotel'. Moreover, she entertained blue-rinse ladies
who appeared miraculously almost as soon as he was
out of the door, and with whom she gossiped about
the glamorous people they read about in wicked
magazines. Her one public defiance was to post in the
window of our house, next to the Vote Labour
sticker, another which advertised the Liberal Party,
so warning the passer-by that ours was a divided
household.

The division became absolute when I passed the
11-plus, and entered High Wycombe Royal Grammar School. My father knew then that I was lost.
RGS had public-school pretensions — with house-
masters, boarders, an Anglican chaplain and cadets.
Soccer had been cancelled in favour of Rugby and
Fives. There was a posh uniform that my parents
could barely afford, and character-forming visits from
Sirs and Colonels and Tory MPs. Jack watched my
progress with impotent rage. I did my best to please
him. I skived off sport, discovered convenient pacifist
convictions which enabled me to opt out of cadets,
and was generally as unhappy and insolent as he
could reasonably have hoped. But he observed the
spiritual transformation which comes about when a
young person is put into proximity with the aristocratic idea. And England, when all is said and done,
was an aristocratic country, whose children were

taught – in the days when they were taught – to be stoical, ironical, and eccentric, conscious of their class but anxious to improve it. When news came that I had gained a scholarship to Cambridge, my father ceased to speak to me except with threats and snarls. Shortly afterwards I ran away from home, took a crash-course in delinquency on the Mile End Road, and ended up penniless and homesick in Lebanon.

This was not a good beginning, but it was the best I could do. Besides, my flight from home had another cause. The England of my father's dreams was not Merry, but chippy and censorious. Nevertheless, it was steeped in pagan ritual, and somewhere in the reaches of his deep emotion the maypole sadly turned, the Morris dancers made desultory tinkles with their bells, and, to the strains of 'Greensleeves', the mud-encumbered clogs were plodding out a dirge. (Incidentally I have observed such rituals only once, in New York, where I came across a street performance by the 'Lower West Side Morris Dancers', whose members were mostly black.) Jack relished the ancient trades which survived in the unscrubbed hollows of our post-war countryside. It cheered him that the cleavers still came to cut the chestnut coppices, so as to sell the wood as 'pale and wire'; he rejoiced that hedgelayers were still employed to bend the may into quickthorn hedges; and even the gypsies in their battered trucks, going from house to house in search of scrap-metal, seemed more real to him than the queues of men each morning at the Thawpit factory.

In those days 'bodgers' lived in makeshift huts in the local woods, turning chair-legs on foot-driven lathes from beech-wood they had hewn and seasoned themselves. The sight of these taciturn and contented old men, with their leather aprons and World War One moustaches, stayed with my father indelibly; they were like beneficent gnomes from an ancient fairy-tale, a glimpse into some deep illumined recess in the collective soul of England. And some of what he felt rubbed off on me.

During my school days a great change came over the world. High Wycombe ceased to be a market town and became a suburb of London. The beech-woods through which I would walk to the Thames at Marlow were sliced in half by a roaring motorway. The furniture trade died off and the bodgers turned their lathes in celestial spheres. The town itself was torn apart: timbered houses gave way to steel-fronted shops; old alleyways where children played hop-scotch were cleared for parking lots; streams were diverted or covered with concrete; faceless blocks rose up with placards declaring 'office space: to let'.

I could hardly dispute my father's version of these events. The town council controlled planning; the Tory Party controlled the council; and the developers controlled the Tory Party, having joined it precisely in order to profit from the destruction of our town. What clearer case could be imagined, of the ruling class against the people? My father devoted the rest of his life to defending the history, townscape and amenities of the place which he had so much loved. I, who had been granted a brief vision of the English countryside, only to see it snatched away and trampled on, retreated to the city, and thence to foreign lands.

The violation of my childhood landscape was an important cause of unhappiness. The troubles at home had led me to reach out for some other, more lasting and more objective image of harmony. I had dreamed the old dream of England, had perceived the 'countenance divine' in our Chiltern valleys, had wandered by the Thames where Stanley Spencer painted, and encountered in those unfrequented country churches, with their 'tense, musty, unignorable silence/ Brewed God knows how long', the lingering presence of a people who had been at one with this landscape and had shaped it through labour and prayer. Eliot, Lawrence and Larkin (whose lines I have just quoted) fed my attachment, and the spreading suburbs with their lawns and lace and garages were like a sentence of death pronounced against my race.

I had also been uplifted by the Prayer Book, which was used in school, and by the hymns that rang out in our Anglican services there. I had even, secretly, in dread not of God's indignation but of Jack's, been confirmed, by a daft old bishop who wondered why my parents were absent on such a happy day. But all this I laid aside in my seventeenth year, like an unfinished meal at the sound of some approaching army.

Lebanon provided my first experience of the Trade

Unions which my father admired. Without money, in a country surrounded by war, I had no option but to work my passage home. The boats were heavily guarded, and each scamper between the gangways might have been my last; but no British ship, however under-manned, would take me, the Seamen's Union having closed the shop. I found a place as deck hand on a Norwegian cargo, which had lost half its improvised crew of sea-sick Canary Islanders in a storm. Arriving in England, I went first to Birmingham, where I read occult books in the city library, and then to Cambridge, to ponder amid the dismal fens an imaginary portrait of my vanished homeland, all the while outdoing my fellow students in loutish behaviour, and escaping when I could to London, parties, drink and girls. In short, I was a typical uncouth grammar-school boy, distinguished from the rest of them by a certain high-toned and literary insolence.

On graduating I went to France, by way of punishing my country for having failed to notice my presence. England did not notice my absence either, and after a brief spell in Italy I crept back to Cambridge, with nothing much to show for my time abroad apart from an unpublishable novel, and the woman who was to be my first wife. Danielle was from the Pyrenees, and could not stomach Cambridge, with its catty dons, its *odium theologicum*, and its air of sanctimonious pederasty. We drifted apart, and then together, and then apart again, marrying and divorcing, rising and sinking on the same

unfathomable seas of anxiety. By the time of our
divorce I had been a don at Cambridge, had become a
University Lecturer in Philosophy in London, had
studied law and was earning extra money as a
conveyancing clerk for a half-mad solicitor whose
clients were Asian sharks.

My thoughts and feelings were dry, trampled,
infertile, and the landscape played no part in them. If,
however, the invitation came to visit a country house,
I would invariably accept, and not only because such
invitations were rare. Everyone condemns snobbery,
but everyone below the Queen is prone to it, even if
only in some inverted form. Almost alone among
great writers, Proust treats the matter honestly. And
he shows us that snobbery after all has an appealing
side: it is a passion that is never reciprocated, a
passion which selflessly expends itself in praise of
those who reward it with contempt. To many people,
brought up without risk or fear or privation, snobbery provides their only path to heroism.

The peculiar thing about country house parties is
that they are exactly like town parties, but with a
background of peacocks and pheasants and rose-
bordered lawns. The same egocentric journalists roll
up at them, and roll out drunk in the midst of
conversation. The same complaisant politicians stand
there amid the hollyhocks and clematis, wearing the
same conceited smiles; the same sequin-spattered
artists, pommaded gallery-directors, wide-eyed
actresses and literary pseuds dance on the lawns,
shattering the air with their squeaky voices, and

poisoning the ancestral pastures with their unscrupulous optimism and relentlessly progressive views. Once or twice I walked through fields and meadows, tramped a grouse moor or learned and then forgot the names of birds. But by and large these visits to the country merely stirred my urban anxiety, presenting me with the same boastful society that I encountered in London – a society in which you had to shine for a while or be snuffed like a flickering candle.

So much for the wretched phase. Out of this wretchedness there at last came a kind of equilibrium. I was unsure that I had talent. But I had energy. So I worked hard to express the thoughts and feelings that occurred to me – and it was a matter of pride to experiment in every medium: philosophy, fiction, essays, journalism. Following divorce, and an unsuccessful attempt at cohabitation, I lived alone in London, growing around myself a polished carapace of learning, teaching in the evenings at Birkbeck College, writing by day, and exploring the avenues of consciousness by night as the great god Bacchus one by one shone his dim light along them. And one of these avenues was politics – not party politics, but the deeper and more troubling thing which centres on a national culture.

The student radicals of France had cured me of socialism. Cambridge had taught me not only to think unpopular things, but also to say them. And the distressing sight of the Tory Party veering towards liberalism prompted me to write of the meaning of conservatism, and of the need to hold on to the national idea – the idea which still slept and dreamed inside me, and which I had not visited since youth.

I was amazed at my success. First my colleagues denounced me; then my students; and very soon just about everyone who was anyone. My books were savaged in the press, my prospects of promotion were blighted, and my acquaintance was confessed to only after long disclaimers and many sad shakes of the head. Obviously, I concluded, there was truth in what I wrote, if people were so anxious to suppress it. And although it was disturbing and frightening to be constantly mocked and vilified, I was encouraged by the small band of fellow conservatives who wrote in support. Like my father, I found my principles – the opposite of his – confirmed in the distress that they caused me.

I came to agree with Nietzsche, that people believe things not because they are true, but because they are fortifying. (But did Nietzsche believe that because it was true, or because it was fortifying?) Ideas, however absurd, gain currency because of the will to believe, and the will to believe is the will to power. For most people the only power available is provided by others: the solution to life's problems, therefore, is to melt into the crowd, and to accept the ruling illusions. That is how the English, once a proud and independent race, became egalitarians. Seeing no hope of power in the robust individualism of their ancestors, they sought power instead in the crowd. In modern England it is dangerous heresy to point out that human beings neither are nor ought to be equal. By writing in such a way you threaten the assumption on which this society of wimps and scroungers is founded.

Still, I was not alone. By now Mrs Thatcher was on the scene, and the very fact that the English (among whom I do not count the Welsh and the Scots) had voted for her suggested that the egalitarian madness might be drawing to an end. It is true that people vote as they think, which is to say they vote for what will strengthen their own position. Still, some ways of strengthening one's position contribute to national revival, and for a while it seemed that Mrs Thatcher's government would do just that. Indeed, the sight of her success was so distressing to my academic colleagues that I, who was manifestly to blame for it, decided that the time had come to leave the university. It took me ten years to accomplish this ambition, since I too was a wimp, and held on to my state-funded salary for as long as it took to achieve a bigger one. But at least I disapproved of this and strove with my pen to put it right.

Public ignominy is a therapy for private guilt: and that is why those years of being sneered at were years of uneasy equilibrium. My mother's death, my father's anger, the trauma of divorce – all had left a residue of contrition and a need for atonement. And atonement came by another way also. Early on in this second period of my life I was invited to give a talk in Prague. The meeting that I addressed was a private one, in a world where each private meeting was a crime. I addressed an assembly of dismissed professors, plain-clothes religious and would-be students on a neutral topic of philosophy. But I saw at once that, in such an environment, no topic is neutral. The impression was confirmed by the secret policeman who hurled me downstairs, and by the strange haunting atmosphere of the streets outside, where no footstep sounded save the footstep close behind, which started and stopped when I did.

This was my first encounter with dissidents. Nothing was of such importance for them, I discovered, as the survival of their national culture. Deprived of material and professional advancement, their days were filled with a forced meditation on their country and its past, and on the question of what it means to be a Czech, trapped in this bounded land-mass, speaking a Slavonic tongue among Germanic peoples, and situated at the very centre of the Christian world. The dissidents were forbidden to publish, and the communists had resolved to remove their traces from the book of history. Hence they were acutely conscious of the value of memory. Their lives were an exercise in what Plato called *anamnesis*: the bringing to consciousness of forgotten things. Something in me responded to this poignant aim, and overnight I became a Czech patriot. I was helped by my need to atone for a confused and selfish life. I was helped by my love of Czech music – and in particular the music of Janáček.

I was helped too by Lenka, the girl whom I met at

the seminar and who gave me my first insights into this place called Absurdistan. I was amazed by what I learned, and ashamed for having played no part in the fight against the communist lie-machine. Thenceforth I devoted all the time I could to supporting my Czech colleagues, to understanding their situation, and to pondering the enigma of Lenka. Her romantic letters came from another spiritual region, a formal garden marked out by saints and monarchs frozen in ecstatic poses, where the spectral voices of Rilke, Zweig, Kafka and von Hofmannsthal still peopled the air, and where all avenues of action led to blank impassable walls. I would visit her in the tiny room she occupied below the hill of Smíchov, and it was as though I entered a familiar dream, a dream where nothing changed and yet where all was provisional. She was *L'Année dernière à Marienbad*, Rusalka and Rilke's angel fused into one.

Lenka married a very angry man; I was arrested and expelled; the world moved on. I continued to work in Eastern Europe, in order to be the greatest possible nuisance to the communist 'authorities', as they called themselves. And I became interested in the mendacity of communist language. For instance, the title of 'authorities' was assumed precisely because everybody, the communists included, knew that they had no authority at all; the communist states called themselves 'people's democracies' because they were not democratic and were built in defiance of the people. It quickly dawned on me that the same inversion of language had infected left-wing movements in the West – where 'social justice' meant robbing those who worked and rewarding those who idled, and where words like 'people', 'society', 'peace', 'caring' and 'class' had the same codified significance as they had acquired under the impact of communist propaganda. The slogans that were spread on the rooftops and balconies of Warsaw and Prague could be found, word for word, in the textbooks of British sociology.

Writing about these things I acquired a new confidence. The angry attacks of my colleagues, I decided, were not my fault but theirs. It was my duty to expose this bunch of frauds and fellow-travellers, and I did so. Being unpopular is never easy; but being unpopular in a good cause is a shield against despair. And gradually, as I thought of those distant friends, keeping the idea of their conquered country alive in the dismal catacombs, I realised that there is another kind of patriotism than the one extolled by Mrs Thatcher – a patriotism of the imagination, which enables you to live, even in the midst of hectic change, among the dead who entrusted their memory to you.

It was in the mid-eighties that my life entered its third and latest phase. I had begun a new career as a journalist, with a column in *The Times* which brought me a wider circle of enemies, and a new circle of friends. One of these friends was Jessica Douglas-Home, who joined me in those anti-communist ventures and fought her own fight against the tide of modern history. Often I went to stay in her house in the Cotswolds, where she — recently widowed, and with two teenage sons — led a quiet and eccentric life among books and ponies and old inherited things. I learned to ride one of her ponies — a low stubby neolithic mongrel called Dumbo, who plodded down country lanes as though treading the unchanging surface of a wheel. Dumbo didn't notice what I noticed in these new surroundings. He didn't notice the dry-stone walls, built from the compact shards of living things, in which the million years of life had left their still living traces. He didn't notice the great trees of cedar and redwood and copper beech which people, in their excess of hopefulness, had planted for the sake of others whom they would neither know nor see. He didn't notice the limestone houses with their stooped and rounded walls like the shoulders of the worn old cottagers who lived in them. To him this tranquil scenery had only one memorable feature, which was that, by treading away at it for long enough, he could cause his stable to reappear on the horizon.

Nevertheless, something of Dumbo's simple love of place was conveyed to me. For the first time since childhood I found myself at home. Admittedly, Dumbo was not my only tutor. Jessica embodied the idea that had flitted across my consciousness in adolescence, teaching me that it is right and just and reasonable to live for vanished things — as my Czech friends lived for vanished things. There was a difference, however. They hoped to restore what they had lost, whereas she knew that our loss and theirs was permanent. We are dying creatures in a dying world. Our place is among the dead, and happiness comes when we acknowledge this, and strive to re-create in imagination, and to some small extent in reality, the moral order that has been established over more than a lifetime for the sake of more than a life.

My rides through the Cotswold countryside were not undertaken in a spirit of nostalgia, however. I loved Jessica's old house precisely because it was a real and living part of the country economy, provid-ing small-scale employment to grooms, gardeners and handymen, cluttered with the débris of genera-tions and distributing its largesse unevenly over a network of friends. It was a fount of hospitality in a world where people still bade each other good morning and stopped to pass the time of day. And each house in the neighbourhood had something of this peaceable and gregarious atmosphere, so that the weird professor and his dung-coloured pony were greeted from doorways and vegetable patches as though they belonged, as trees and sheep belong, with the unseen throbbing movement of the seasons.

Nearby lived Laurie Lee, author of a book that had deeply affected my father when, in later life, books began to impress him. *Cider with Rosie* lovingly unfolds the Cotswold landscape, with its flora and fauna and people, as an antiquarian unrolls a vellum map. But, while it was no part of its author's intention, the book joined the ever-growing pile of 'heritage', making its own small but significant

contribution to the process whereby rural life has
been slowly emptied of its economic entrails and
preserved as a varnished skin. This exercise in moral
taxidermy may look harmless when compared with
the vast and thoughtless ventures into the future
which are motorways and high-rise office blocks. It
became apparent to me, however, as it was not
apparent to Dumbo – horses being conservative, but
only in the unimaginative way which rejects all
innovation – that the heritage idea is but one among
many aspects of the motor industry. The force which
had set the world in motion, driving highways hither
and thither for no other purpose than to reach places
rendered uniformly dull by the ease of reaching them,
which had poisoned the towns, demolished their
centres and driven the people to the suburbs, which
had reorganised the entire economy around the
manufacture of machines – and machines of a peculiar
kind, which were not so much used as *consumed* – this
very same force had packaged the remaining fragments of real life and sold them off as 'heritage', to be
visited, gawped at and swallowed from the inside of a
motor car.

Only if people dwell in the land, rooted there from
generation to generation, does its ancestral quality
become apparent. You can verify this by a simple
experiment. Visit first a major country house main-
tained by the National Trust, with all its contents
carefully catalogued and displayed in authentic surroundings. Your curiosity will be aroused, and you
will be granted a vision of vanished grandeur and

elevated style. But it will be a frame from a moving picture, frozen for ever in the posture of death: ancient but not ancestral, since incapable of breeding.

Visit now a minor country house like Jessica's — a house still inhabited by the family, with its furniture much broken and much repaired, its undistinguished portraits and smokey sylvan scenes, its bustle of life and clamour of voices, its cluttered corridors and piled-up attic — and you will receive an impression which is in many ways the opposite. These objects, which would be of no interest whatsoever in a museum, are warm, friendly, bathed in the light of ownership, a smiling and shifting background to the reproduction of human life. The atmosphere is ancestral, not ancient, and the charm and beauty of the surroundings speak directly of renewal — renewal of a house, a landscape, and a way of life.

Taxes on wealth and inheritance are a seemingly inevitable feature of democratic politics. Hence one by one all country houses will either disintegrate or be preserved by the National Trust as mausoleums. The same could happen to the countryside, though for different reasons. It will happen as soon as people cease to remake the countryside through the process of their own reproduction. If you love the hedgerows and pastures, the patchwork of fields, the copses and coverts* which lie scattered among them, and the

---

* Space does not permit me to ponder the strange hunting idiolect. But this word needs explaining. It is in fact the French *couvert*. The 't' is therefore not pronounced, though retained in

footpaths, bridleways and hunt jumps which allow
the passage through, then it is because you see in
these things the imprint of human life. Ancestral
patterns of ownership and labour speak to us from
our landscape – patterns which have been wiped
away from the industrialised prairies of East Anglia,
as they have been wiped away from the collective
farms of Russia, Hungary and Bohemia. In the hedge-
seamed tapestry of the English pasture, you can read
the history of the land and those who have lived in it.
This landscape was made for a human use, and
without its use it will lose its beauty.

Many of the occupations that kept people on the
land have disappeared. While created by work, the
landscape is destined for leisure. And yet, if the
leisure does not involve those who live and work in
rural areas, the landscape will cease to be theirs and
become a theme-park for suburban visitors. The cities
will then become places of migration, in which people
no longer dwell, since dwelling requires piety,
obedience and the sense of community. Like the cities
of North America, they will turn into waste-lands of
violence and crime, from which people flee to the
expanding suburbs, there to exist in a kind of moral
and aesthetic limbo. In that world without neighbourliness, without the earth and its warm attach-
ments – that world of metalled roads, Astro-turf and
'Executive Homes' from a builder's catalogue – the

the spelling, in order to emphasize that the thing which covers
the fox is also the place where he covertly moves.

New Man will live out his days in tinsel-spattered
isolation, knowing the outside world only through
the windscreen of his motor car, and adding with
every unnecessary journey to the cloud of gas which
one day will stifle us all.

Such thoughts often troubled me on my rural
rides. And it was while meditating on the Potemkin
economy that is rotting our countryside that I
discovered hunting. We were clopping down a
narrow lane between grass verges, on one side a vast
stretch of ugly 'set-aside', on the other a vaster field
of winter barley. It was a raw November day, and the
bleak brown furrows glimmered beneath scratchy
aluminium clouds, the hedgeless ditches like the
trenches of some recent battle-front. Even in the
Cotswolds you encounter these Brussels-blighted
regions, where boundaries, coverts and spinneys have
been razed and pastures ploughed for the sake of
subsidies. And while Dumbo plodded on, expecting
his stable to loom into view with food and warmth
and safety, I pondered the wasted land and felt my
hopes of home again receding. Perhaps I should have
kept to my old routines – encountering England only
in literature, and taking my rural rides with William
Cobbett.

Those gloomy thoughts had begun to take hold of
me, when Dumbo stopped in his tracks and pricked
his ears. I kicked him, and kicked again. He would
not budge. Nor did the stick interrupt for more than
a second his deep concentration. He had raised his
head and turned it slightly to one side, scanning the

grey horizon. And there, after a moment, I made out a strange commotion.

A mottled cream-coloured dog was running along the edge of the field, nose to the ground and tail wagging. It dropped into a ditch and rose at once on the other side; another dog came after it, and then another. And after a moment there reached me across the sticky waste the sound that Dumbo, with his acuter ears, had heard already – the musical baying of foxhounds, as they pick up a scent. The pack had swollen now to a dozen or more, swarming out of the dim horizon like bees from a hidden hollow. And then came the excited stammer of the huntsman's horn – a repeated tonguing on one note which recalled the earth dance from the *Rite of Spring*. Stravinsky may have been an armchair anthropologist, but his music touches something deep in the species, the very dance of death and regeneration which was skirting the wet ditches of this blighted farm-land, and bringing it against the odds to life.

The head of a horse came nodding over the horizon, pulling on the viscous air and levering its rider into view across the field: a wiry, red-jacketed figure with a leathery red face, who was leaning forward in the saddle, horn pressed to lips, cheeks pumping like bellows. Soon he was cantering along the ditch, the pack of hounds running gleefully beside him, the horse eager and untroubled amid its ancient foes. They leapt a ditch, and disappeared downhill, the horn stuttering in semi-quavers, the hounds in full cry along the soggy furrows.

Throughout this performance Dumbo had
remained stock still, ears forward and eyes fixed on
the passing dance. Nor did he move as the sound
receded. Still my kicks were ignored, and still his feet
seemed rooted to the tarmac. Only in one particular
did he change: his ears swivelled back on their roots
like radar-scanners, searching for some other sound.
Long before I heard it he had begun to roll his eyes
backwards and turn his head. And then, from
somewhere behind us, came the distant ring of
hooves on metalled roadway, the crossing rhythms of
a collective canter, the subdued din of approaching
cavalry.

Before I could take stock of the situation, we were
in the midst of the herd. Seventeen-hand horses were
snorting and heaving to every side, their buttocks
rippling with muscle like the seething wakes of ocean
liners; a man in a red coat was shouting 'hold hard';
fierce women in mud-spattered uniforms were cantering past me with intent and angry faces. Dumbo
meanwhile had suffered a metamorphosis as far-
fetched as any in Ovid. His neck was arched, his head
down, with the bit held firmly in his teeth; his feet
were dancing on the road, and great surges of life
rose through his quarters, invading and inflaming me
on their way to his heart and his head. He had
rediscovered his life. As when a fish, rescued from the
riverbank where it lies motionless and staring, is
thrown back into water and instantly swims, so did
Dumbo, dropped into the herd from a state of
suspended animation, become what he truly is, and

what he had never been for me. Soon we were cantering down the road with the rest of them, the man in the red coat shouting, and others laughing beside me and cheering me on.

The first thing that became apparent was that I had not known before what a horse really is. I was not riding an individual; I was borne up with my fellows on the waves of the herd. Dumbo was one cell in the organism which contained and swamped him. The few equestrian skills that I had mastered were of no effect in guiding or controlling this creature, who had ceased to be a quiet station where nothing changed, and become a busy junction, through which express trains of horsey passion rushed from every point, thundering onwards to destinations far beyond the perimeter of Dumbo.

The second thing that I understood was that Dumbo, despite his diminutive size and sedentary life, was a 'front-runner', a horse determined to be first in the herd. As soon as the stampede had quietened, he began to push his way forward, thrusting between the forbidding thighs of horses twice his stature, emerging at last, to the great amusement of my new companions, beside the man in red, proudly holding up his snorting head as self-appointed leader of the field.

The third thing that I understood was that this seething chaos of horse-flesh was not a chaos at all, but a closely disciplined cavalry, bound by rules of etiquette and combat, and that the black coat, top boots, white stock and breeches were not fancy dress,

but the insignia of office, as vital to discipline as is a
soldier's uniform. The man in red, I learned, was the
Field Master, the officer in charge, and only my
status as a rank outsider freed me, as I barged in
front of him, from the charge of insubordination.

Like most sheltered intellectuals, I knew hunting
only from literature: from Fielding's portrait of
Squire Western, from cross-country scrambles in
Trollope, and from Macaulay's icy dismissal of the
gentry in his *History of England*. Insofar as hunting
survived, I assumed, it was the province of rich
Londoners whose city-nurtured need for whipping
and killing brought them out into the countryside
with rage in their faces and death in their hearts.

The reality surprised me. The Master, I discovered, was a farmer, one who spoke with a broad
Wiltshire accent, and whose easy and demotic
manner recalled the pub, the barbecue and the skittle
alley rather than the boardroom or the country
house. He addressed me with friendly and apologetic
words, and held Dumbo's bridle as I dismounted. We
had reached the brow of a hill, and the huntsman and
hounds could be seen in the valley below, moving
through pasture beside a meandering stream.
Another horse was with them, ridden also by a man
in red – the whipper-in, as I later learned. The
hounds were no longer baying, and the huntsman's
horn was silent. Often I had ridden through this
valley, since the road led back to Jessica's, and a
bridleway skirted the stream. But never before had it
seemed so tranquil and removed. The down-turned

eager noses of the hounds, the easy posture of the huntsman as he quietly encouraged them, and the gently trotting horses as they moved in step with the pack, were hung on a single thread of life, as though they took their being from the pastures, and as though something flowed between them and through them from the very place where they were. This ordinary piece of England was here, now and always.

Of course, I was familiar with hunting prints, with lampshades, table mats and tea-trays celebrating 'the sport of our ancestors'. And being a mere intellectual, I had dismissed them as mass-produced kitsch. But what I observed was neither kitsch nor cliché. There by the willow-cumbered banks I saw the moving image of eternity. Here was an unselfconscious union between species, which was also a rejoicing in the land. It was neither Nature nor Heritage nor any other marketed thing. It was, like God, too shy and true for marketing, as inward and secret and comforting as soul is, and as durable. I know this more clearly now, in retrospect. But I sensed it then, and a strange apprehension came over me, like falling in love – the apprehension of the self taken hostage by an outside force.

On that winter morning in a Cotswold valley, faced with an image which had been traded in a thousand times at the counter of false sentiment, I saw that image and reality diverge. I did not grasp what was happening in the valley; I did not understand why the huntsman blew his horn and took the hounds in another direction, or why the other horseman galloped towards the copse that crowned the hill. But I knew that the valley no longer slept in the dream of Heritage. It had been lifted down from the rack of Cotswold postcards and was once again alive, as it had been alive down the centuries whenever visited by this drama. The snorting horses and eager people behind me were part of the event: though why the Master held them back, and why he bid them be silent, were also matters that escaped me.

By now I had led Dumbo to one side, and was edging down the road towards the turning which would take us home. Suddenly the huntsman's horn stuttered out its excited semi-quavers. The hounds, which had been drifting around the trotting horse like gulls around a fishing boat, instantly formed a line, running one behind the other towards the copse, each hound breaking into song as it jumped the low stone wall that crossed the valley. There was a commotion behind me. I turned to see the Master swing his horse towards the rails that bordered the road on this side of the valley and then rush at them with a scraping of hooves. The other riders followed, some forty or more, each horse fired with enthusiasm, pulling its rider into the jump, and following the herd in its downhill stampede towards the river, into which they plunged like the Gadarene swine. Dumbo was rearing in my hand, and I was tempted to let him go. But soon the hunt had waded the shallow steam, had galloped off behind the copse and was lost to view. Dumbo allowed me to mount him for the journey home, setting off at once at an excited trot, ears pricked, eyes searching the horizon to every side, hoping for the miraculous vision to be granted again. Only when the familiar houses of his village lined the road, did he return to his plodding gait. And I noticed then that he was drooping and covered in sweat.

Thus it was that I resolved to take up hunting during this, the best part of my life. The next ten years were given to fulfilling that ambition, along with two others: to be employed by no-one, and to live by my wits. The three ambitions were really one and the same: I was taking a step back from the modern world into a realm of ancestral freedoms. I was also discovering England.

CHAPTER TWO

Beginning

It is not easy to start hunting. Of course, you can follow the hunt on foot or by car, and I was surprised to learn how many people did so. But to do the thing properly you need a horse, and not just any horse – a horse that will go fast and sure across country, taking in jumps as they come. You need to ride that horse, which means staying on and also stopping it. And you need the proper dress, hunting being one of the few pursuits for which formal dress is still compulsory.

There are four grades of hunt costume: 'rat-catcher', the black hunting coat, the special colours or buttons of the hunt, and the uniforms of the masters and servants. Incidentally, hunting is also one of the few pursuits in which the words 'master' and 'servant' have retained their traditional use. Elsewhere they have been replaced by 'employer' and 'employee' – euphemisms which empty the most important of all economic ties of its meaning and history.

Rat-catcher is worn by children, by beginners and by the entire hunt during the long pre-amble to the season – the time of cub-hunting, when efforts are devoted to culling and dispersing the fox-population, rather than to sport. It consists of a tweed jacket of muddy complexion, grey or brown breeches, brown boots and either a sober tie or a coloured stock. The black hunting coat is the correct wear for the season, and must be accompanied by white breeches, boots (preferably leather top boots), white stock, gloves and top hat or hunting cap. Because hunts are jealous of their privileges, however, the full colours are reserved for those who have earned them. At a certain point, and for reasons entirely mysterious to the newcomer, the committee of the hunt will invite you to wear its insignia. As with another famous cavalry exploit, yours not to reason why. Time, of course, has something to do with it – time which heals the wounded feelings of the herd. But time is not the most important factor. The hunt is one of the few communities which has retained 'rites of passage': it offers grades of membership, each marked out by some ceremonial display. Some hunts honour their inner circle with buttons only – such is the VWH (Vale of White Horse) to which I first belonged. Others, like the Beaufort Hunt next door, have special coloured jackets as their badge of membership (in this case the celebrated 'blue and buff'). Finally masters and hunt-servants wear a distinguishing livery – the traditional 'hunting pink'* for the

---

* So-called, they say, not for its colour, but because originally provided by Mr Pink, tailor, of Jermyn Street. In fact the red

VWH, a cheerful bottle-green for the Beaufort.

I mention these details because dress codes are almost universally misunderstood, and because they are both part of the appeal of hunting and one of the secret reasons why people are opposed to it. Since the dawn of time men have hunted. And when they cease to hunt by necessity, and turn instead to the plough, they continue to hunt by choice. Hunting then becomes a ceremony, an act of communion, a part of courtliness and kingship. For civilised man hunting is not a hobby but a symbol of leisure, freedom and abundance. Like dancing, it is done for no other purpose, yet done in company; and, like dancing (or at least, dancing of the old-fashioned kind), it is filled with celebration.

That is why costume is so much a part of it. You dress for hunting not merely as a courtesy to the farmer over whose land you intend to gallop, but also because you are rising to an occasion. Dressing places ritual and ceremony at the centre of society, where they belong. Egalitarians dislike this. Through ceremonial dress people show their respect for rules, offices and hierarchies, and recreate the image of courtliness. The ceremonial uniform is a supreme example of man's ability to represent himself as descended from a higher sphere; and although its

---

hunting coat is usually a bright scarlet, and probably derives from the cavalry uniform worn by the officers of Wellington's army during the Peninsular War, the Duke having brought a pack of foxhounds with him to the Pyrenees.

effect is precisely to make all distinctions irrelevant, except the distinction between the one who does, and the one who does not wear the costume, it is a rebuff to the modern idea of equality, which would make all life a playground, with the bullies in charge.

In 'A Prayer for my Daughter', Yeats asks a rhetorical question:

> How but in custom and in ceremony
> Are innocence and beauty born?

I don't know. But I *do* know that innocence and beauty are present in the hunt, and that custom and ceremony are part of their cause. And the ceremony extends to the horse, whose appearance is governed by a code as exacting as that which governs the dress of his rider. The saddle must be clean and soaped and polished, shining at the cantle and framed by a fleecy numnah. Special tack is added – breastplate, standing martingale, and leather girth – each piece soaped and polished to a lithe and living thing. While such bits and bobs are far from useless, but on the contrary adopted for safety's sake, they have the ornamental character of all things that are worn against the body. Hence we fit and adjust them with high enthusiasm, just as our ancestors caparisoned their steeds. Almost all animals look ridiculous in clothes. The one exception is the horse, whose loveliness is of a piece with the loveliness of silk and velvet.

The attention given to his covering, however, is nothing to that expended on the horse. Clipped and

dandy-brushed, his coat lies on his limbs like French
polish on a table, glowing with autumn colours, and
scattered with precincts of light. His hooves are
anointed with sweet-smelling oil and shine like
polished tortoiseshell. His mane is plaited and laid
flat, so that the neck is revealed in its glory; his tail is
picked and cropped and plaited up, so that the rear
end is no less noble than the fore. (Much has been
written about the posterior of horses, about their
sweet-smelling ordure and their unique ability neither to embarrass nor disgust us with their bodily
functions – facts which clearly inspired Swift in his
amiable portrait of the Houyhnhnms. But not enough
has been said in praise of the tail, which continues the
noble line that stretches from the head along the
back, and flares out in triumph like a flag of fortune,
waving always goodbye as it conquers the land.)

In his treatise on horsemanship Xenophon
remarked on the resemblance between the pride of
humans and that of horses. Our two species share a
need to move in groups, and at the same time to draw
attention to themselves as glamorous individuals –
arching and extending their limbs, so as to magnetise
the space surrounding them. When we sit on a horse
we are judged as one half of a centaur; hence our
concern with appearances receives an added boost
from these animals who mimic our social instincts.
We enter the field with a share of their excitement,
returning to our tribal existence as they return to the
herd, eager like them to be wholly part of it while
remaining uniquely ourselves.

That is why the costume of the hunt, for all its local variations, is really a uniform. It is often said that people look more distinguished in uniform. For a uniform is a frame: it challenges us to become more emphatically ourselves. But it also defines a station in life and the duties that go with it. Hunt dress creates a kind of distinction-in-uniformity — an equality of individuals, far removed from the identity-in-drabness which is the norm in city streets.

There are those for whom nothing is more dispiriting than pressing a stud against a choking Adam's apple, squeezing agonized thighs into breeches and shins into shrivelled leather boots. For hunting people, however, the hours of preparation are the necessary prelude to their festive day. Each detail has, for them, its own peculiar meaning, as I discovered when I caused Jessica to unearth and explain to me the hunting gear that her father had worn, and which was stored in the family attic along with generations of eccentric débris — the spiritual leaf-mould of a tribe. The silver-plated button-hook with its carved ivory handle; the fluted buttons and leather shin-straps; the obstinate boots and spurs which refuse to navigate the heel; the itchy braces, fastened to finger-bruising buttons of brass, which require you to dismantle the whole structure at the call of nature; the shrunken white gloves, showing blotches of constricted flesh; the studs which press, stocks which strangle and stock-pins which pierce the throat — these things, which for many are instruments of torture, are, I discovered, symbols of a sacred ritual, the more venerated the older and tougher they are.

The rat-catcher which Jessica unearthed was a very bad fit. But it sufficed for the level of smartness appropriate to Dumbo. By paying a small cap (small since Dumbo hardly counted as a horse) I gained permission to follow. And so it was that, on a wet December day ten years ago, I had my first experience of hunting. Of course, I would not jump, since neither I nor Dumbo, I believed, could manage it. Nor would I gallop over difficult terrain or embark on one of those 'ten-mile points' that I had read about in the hunting literature lying in a rarely visited corner of Jessica's drawing room. My intention was to potter at a distance, a visiting anthropologist who was no part of the tribe. Besides, a professor on a fourteen-hand pony should do his best to be inconspicuous.

Dumbo's views did not coincide with mine. Already, hacking to the meet, and passed on the road by trailers issuing their horsey sounds and smells, he knew that 'something was afoot'. (An idiom that we owe, as we owe so many, to hunting.) Glimpsing other horses on the road before us, his brisk trot turned to a canter; by the time we reached the pub where the hunt was assembled, he was bathed in sweat and cantering on the spot in his excitement.

I cannot say what was most thrilling or surprising about the meet. Was it the hounds, gathered in a circle around their god and master, eyes fixed on his, urging him with tail and tongue to get a move on?

Was it the huntsman, with his tanned leather face and canny eyes, his frame set deep in the saddle as though rooted there? Was it the mounted followers, so spick and span and crisply uniformed, drowning anxiety in the landlord's gin and ginger? Was it the many more who had gathered on foot, the villagers, farmers, terrier men and foot-followers – the social foundation on which this exultant edifice was built? Was it perhaps the ritualised politeness – the doffing of caps, the hearty 'good-mornings', the bowing and nodding and acknowledging which have all but disappeared from city ways, but which provide such warmth and comfort to the visiting stranger? Or was it just the extraordinary atmosphere – that inimitable mixture of holiday excitement and battle-field nerves which makes the meet so necessary a preliminary to hunting? I cannot say. But I *can* say that my life was changed by the experience. For once I was not observing from afar. Here was a piece of England which was not yet alien to itself, a community which had yet to be ground into atoms and scattered as dust. I was witnessing innocent and unaffected membership, a corporate smile as spontaneous as the wagging tails of the hounds and the pricked ears of the horses. And I wanted to join.

In this at least Dumbo's feelings and mine coincided. When, with a sharp toot of the horn and a cry of 'Hounds please!', the pack began to move, an electric thrill of anticipation shot through Dumbo's body. Before I could see where we were going, he was pushing between the great haunches of the herd,

obstinately seeking the front. Soon he was in the
midst of the avant-garde, the bit firmly held between
his teeth, his neck arched and determined. To my
alarm we turned off the road into a river, and the
great splashing horses to either side threw sheets of
cold water across us. Dumbo was delighted, and
began to stamp his feet in the water, to indignant
female cries. This was my first encounter with what I
came to know in time as the only real terror of the
hunt: the hunting schoolma'am, a fierce implacable
creature specializing in strict lessons, who could
never advertise them, however, in a London phone-
box. More of her later.

We emerged from the stream into water meadows,
and were soon cantering down a muddy bridle-way
flanked by fences and trees. I was astonished by the
sticky quality of the mud that was flying through the
air. The manicured centaurs of a moment before were
now heaving hippopotami, creatures of the alluvial
bog, their elegance gone beneath a dribbling film of
brown slime. All those hours of preening and
polishing had been undone in a moment. But the
sight was enchanting. Through this negation of our
labours nature completes them, showing that their
purpose lies in no advantage but only in themselves.
In hunting nothing is merely a means, but everything
an end in itself; here, pouring down the track in
cheerful cavalcade, myself a timorous part of it, was
Kant's Kingdom of Ends – the community which is
nowhere and everywhere, the eternally recurring
glimpse of our transcendental home.

Gladly, however, would I have left the fray, so as to observe it from amphitheatrical heights. For although Dumbo was lagging, he would not relinquish the bit, and responded not at all to my pleas for caution. Something was happening in front, a pausing and heaving and grunting that dreadfully alarmed me. One by one we were to pass some test or ordeal, and surely I would be disgraced, dismounted, thrown, mutilated, killed. Before I had diagnosed the danger it was visible, just a few yards away: a post and rail at which the great black gelding in front of us was hurling itself like an angry dog at a rabbit. As the gelding rose in the air so did my heart rise into my mouth, with the 'me next' feeling of the prisoner lined up for torture. Dumbo was already plunging when the rail, hit by the gelding's mighty forelegs, splintered noisily and scattered across the meadow, the horse cantering on regardless with its rider clinging to its neck. Such strokes of fortune are rare and unpredictable. I resolved, therefore, as Dumbo galloped through the gap, to take him away from this stampede of lunatics and watch the show from afar.

The horses came to a halt in the sopping grassland, and I calmed my nerves in talk. I was surprised by the kindness of my fellow horsemen, and by their open acceptance of a wimpish amateur on a pony. I was soon to learn that this acceptance was illusory. Nevertheless, I rejoiced at the even temper of my hosts (for so I regarded them), and even confessed to being a hopeless rider, whose principal intention was to stay out of trouble on the roadway.

'Don't do that,' said my neighbour – a brick-faced
farmer with a squint, who eyed me curiously as
though trying to ascertain to what species I belonged
– 'or you'll head the fox.'

'Then maybe I'll go round the other side of the
wood there,' I ventured.

'Not without the Master's permission you won't,'
came the gruff reply.

It was soon borne in on me that I had no
alternative but to stay with the 'field' (as the mounted
followers are collectively called). If I kept my cool,
however, there was no need to jump, and I could stay
at the back with the gate-shutters. Staying at the
back was easier said than done. Thankfully, however,
no fox was found in the spinney by the water
meadows, and, with a few brisk toots of the horn the
huntsman called out the hounds. We set off at a trot
towards the gravel pits. Dumbo was already calmer,
my confidence was returning, and I began to observe
this curious society in a more relaxed frame of mind.

In so far as hunting had been touched on in Jack
Scruton's narrative of England, it was as an occupa-
tion of the landed gentry, a brazen advertisement of
power and money and class, designed to intimidate
the peasantry by trampling on their crops, with the
added advantage that an innocent animal would be
brutally killed in the process. Even if there had once
been some truth in that idea, it was true, I perceived,
no longer. The mounted followers of the VWH
contained a few people who spoke with toffee-noses,
but they were on terms of equality with the

remainder, and manifestly deferred to those in the know. 'Those in the know' were sent out on 'point' to the corners of coverts, there to watch for the emerging fox. They included farmers, servicemen, a fishmonger, a scrap-metal merchant, several house-wives, and children too – for there is no better sensor of the hounds, no better 'reflector' as Henry James would put it, of those quiet, dogged urgencies in the hidden undergrowth, than a fox-hunting child, a child who grew into animals as a tree into soil, outside the nursery, and without the corrupting mulch of Disneyland.

Many of the followers were people far poorer than I, forced to borrow a horse, or to hack along on some backyard pony whose every hunt may be the last – or rather, the last but one, it being an act of piety among hunting people to give their condemned horses to the kennels, so that they may have one last run across country in the bellies of the hounds. Some devote all their time and wealth and energy to the care of a singe hunter; others – the minority – keep several magnificent animals, and a groom who delivers them, one to the meet at 11 a.m., and another to 'second horses' at 2, and who puts them to bed at the end of the day.

What quickly becomes apparent to the newcomer, however, is that the mounted followers compose only a fraction of the hunt. Half the country participates, crawling in cars along narrow lanes. Many trudge on foot through fields and hedgerows, and in time their forms and faces become familiar, popping from the

undergrowth whenever there is a lull in the battle.
These foot-followers are the psychic core of the hunt,
the people closest to the land and to the creatures
who live in it, the ones without wealth or pretension,
who look on the huntsman with the same passionate
trust as do the hounds. Some of them are young, and
the VWH is usually accompanied across country by
day labourers, apprentice electricians, mechanics, and
sturdy girls in gumboots. Alas, however, many more
are old: retired farmhands and shepherds in tattered
gaberdines, their precious terriers cradled in their
arms; fierce farming widows in tweed and string; and
strange gnomes risen inexplicably from the bowels of
the earth, like the ancient, brittle-haired enthusiast in
a tattered coat of black worsted who, supporting
himself on knobbly sticks and with a red face scoured
like a joint of pork by his journeys through the
hedgerows, emerges now behind and now in front of
the horses, his ratty eyes darting from side to side,
his white knuckles shaking in vulpicidal rage.

The foot-followers are old not because hunting is a
dying pursuit – far from it – but because the rural
economy, dehumanized by subsidies, makes no place
for the young. Our situation approaches that
lamented by Goldsmith in 'The Deserted Village':

> Ill fares the land to hast'ning ills a prey,
> Where wealth accumulates, and men decay;
> Princes and lords may flourish, or may fade;
> A breath can make them as a breath has made;
> But a bold peasantry, their country's pride,

When once destroy'd can never be supplied.

Not quite however. For the 'bold peasantry' are still there at each meet, and assembled again at the end of each day, their faces shining with exhilaration, as human faces always shine when something futile has been done supremely well.

My first day on Dumbo gave me only a smattering of such information – but enough, all the same, to show me that I had fallen into one of the most curious societies that survive from the lost pre-modern age of human virtue. As yet the work of the hounds remained a mystery, and although, when they began to 'speak' at the next covert, I was as excited by the sound as my neighbours, I could not under-stand why we waited, long after the baying had dwindled in some distant corner. My neighbours fell silent and stared away from each other, their ears cocked, their faces tense with expectation. And then, loud and long and horrible, there sounded from the far side of the covert a blood-curdling cry. It was like the moment in Strauss's *Elektra*, when Orestes, intent on vengeance, has entered the palace of his mother, and a long sinister murmuring in the orchestra is suddenly broken by Clytaemnestra's dying screams. This dreadful sound, I learned, was a 'halloa' (pro-nounced 'holla'), sent up by a local farmer's wife, who was on point at the far side of the wood. It meant that the fox had emerged from hiding, and was fleeing for his life across the meadows.

Even so we did not move. For another halloa

sounded from the opposite direction. Then another
from further afield, and another. The country was
staked out between these shafts of sound, tense as a
drum on which a god was beating. Never before had I
heard the landscape come alive like this; for although
I had often woken in the room above the mill-race at
Jessica's to the song of birds and the plash of running
water, these noises entered my ears like sound effects,
radio-producer's short-hand for 'somewhere out of
town', and most other country sounds belong to the
cacophonous chorus of the mechanized farm: tractors,
earth-movers, bird-scarers, milking machines.

There being several foxes afoot, I learned, the
huntsman must decide which to follow; hence the
rapid patter – the doubling of the horn – with which
he summoned the hounds as he galloped along the
border of the covert. He passed through an open gate,
into a field where a horseman had raised his hat and
now pointed with it across the pasture. As they
crossed the place, the hounds one by one sang out, a
long wavering high note, always at the same pitch,
an involuntary expression of thoughts too deep for
variation. And there recurred that miraculous and
instant transformation of the pack which I had
already witnessed: the change from a crowd of
cheerful hooligans to a disciplined line of soldiers,
running one behind the other on the trail of the fox.
The chase that followed was reportedly one of the
best recorded. I did not see it, however. All attempts
to stay at the back met with failure, and within
minutes Dumbo, wheezing like a steam train, was

dragging me towards a fence over which the Pega-
sus-feet of flying cavalry had a moment previously
soared. A few seconds later I was leaning against a
tree, winded and confused, with the jubilant Dumbo
galloping across the field beyond, stirrups flapping at
his sides like wings, flying over a post and rail, and
disappearing round a corner in the wake of the herd.
Jessica's old boots, I discovered, as I trudged through
the soggy field, let in copious floods of water, and no
field is more dreary or forbidding than that from
which the hunt has disappeared, taking one's horse
along with it. By the time Dumbo was brought back
to me by a far from happy gate-shutter, I had decided
to call it a day.

Like all people who live at the taxpayer's expense,
university teachers think they are paid too little. My
own view is that, with the exception of those who
could never be adequately rewarded, since they
inspire the love of learning in the young, university
teachers are paid too much. Still, even with my
second career as a journalist, I was not well off, and
would be hard pressed to pay for the clothes, the
horse, the hunt subscription and the livery, all of
which would be essential to this pursuit which was
now essential to me.

Chance again came to my rescue. Five years
previously I had begun to edit, under the auspices of
a discussion group dedicated to the philosophy of
Lord Salisbury (that great prime minister whose
greatness consists precisely in the fact that no-one
knows anything about him), a quarterly magazine of

conservative thought. *The Salisbury Review* was the
target of much abuse from those whose morality
forbad them to read it, and in 1987 I won the first of
several libel actions – this one against the BBC. With
£2,500 in my pocket I was able to think about
buying a horse.

The *Review* celebrated its fifth anniversary with a
dinner, at which Enoch Powell was the guest of
honour, and since I had to introduce the Right
Honourable gentleman, I sat next to him. Intimidat-
ing people are not many, but Enoch Powell was one
of them. The constant sideways glances from his
steely eyes seemed to express a suspicion that he had
turned up at the wrong dinner, and that I was trying
without success to make a fool of him. At the same
time he radiated a deep and absolutist conviction on
every topic that I touched on, leaving a short silence
in the wake of his robust paragraphs, into which, it
was implied, I was free to stuff my disagreement. His
speech, with its level intonation, Victorian syntax and
biblical turns of phrase, belonged with those ancestral voices of Coleridge, prophesying war even while
welcoming the pudding. And he gave a distinct
impression that present company was no more than
temporary – that he might at any moment be lifted
by divine intervention from this world of fools to take
his former place among the angels.

Matters were made worse by the fact that I
admired him. He was one of the few politicians for
whom England was still the centre of the world.

Even if there was something mournful and valedic-
tory in his vision of our country, there was also a
wilful, Nelsonian scorn — the kind of scorn of the
timid and the ordinary that had saved us in the past
and might save us again. He was free of small-talk.
Whenever an escape-route appeared in the wall of
trivia, his conversation would veer away into sublim-
ities, and the components of British politics — the
crown, the common law, the lords and commons —
appeared in his discourse not as humdrum collections
of modern people but as radiant and transfiguring
ideas, which shone above the course of history and
cast their great light along the centuries.

Long before the pudding appeared, my inability to
say anything new on Wagner, Nietzsche or Aeschy-
lus had been conclusively established. As the time for
speeches neared, I decided to make one last sally, and
to speak about what really interested me. At the
mention of fox-hunting, Enoch laid down his fork,
and looked at me long and hard, with eyes which had
lost their glassy remoteness, and burned with a living
fire. He seemed to be noticing me for the first time, as
he poured out a confiding flow of memories. Enoch
had been a keen follower in his day, and hunting with
hounds was for him not only integral to the identity
of our kingdom, but also something of profound,
almost metaphysical, significance. He spoke of Homer
and Xenophon, of Swinburne and Trollope, and
painted a romantic picture of Northern Ireland from
which I gathered that the Unionist cause is in some
mystical way continuous with the survival of classical

civilization and that the connecting link is to be found in hunting.

Seeming convinced by now that I was neither a spoof nor an impostor but an apprentice member of the very angelic host that had dispatched him on his mission to the English, Enoch finally addressed me with a question: 'Are you not the same basic size, physically, if not mentally, as I?' – such was its gist. Without waiting for my answer, he offered to sell, at rock bottom price, the hunting costume which lay unused in his chest of drawers at home. 'Only one owner and good as new.' The offer was irresistible. A week later I emerged from a small but elegant house near Sloane Square, carrying a pair of hunting boots with mahogany-coloured tops and spurs, and a black coat which – though somewhat tight at the chest, notwithstanding the indignation which had once so magnificently swelled in it – compared favourably with the coats that I had seen at the VWH.

To be correctly dressed is pointless, however, if you have no horse to sit on. And good horses are hard to find. First, you need advice, and the person advising you is very likely to be making money on the deal. When I let it be known that my maximum was £2,500, I was advised to spend it on George, who, by a wondrous chance, cost exactly that amount. He was a bay gelding, described thus: 17 hands 2 inches, quiet, experienced hunter, one lady rider, nine years old. I have since learned to decipher such descriptions, in which only one detail – the height – can be easily verified. And in George's case

this one detail was frightening. As for the rest, here is
what it means: has not yet bitten his groom, has done
far too much work, maybe even a bit of hunting, has
had unknowably many riders, and is at least fifteen.
(Big horses tend to die before they are twenty.) But I
was desperate for a horse, and was assured that this
fierce creature, who set off at full speed the moment I
sat on him, suffered from nothing worse than a sense
of humour. I bought him, spent a summer learning to
ride him, and decided that, although he did have a
tendency to bolt across open country; although he
would often stop dead, rear up on his hind legs, and
gallop back to his stable; although he frequently
baulked at obstacles and then jumped from a stand-
still, so guaranteeing my ejection from the saddle, all
these faults were really mine and that, as time went
on and I learned to handle him, George would prove
docile, reliable and kind.

I was right in that judgement, and George went on
hunting until he was (by the vet's estimate) a good
twenty-seven years old. And my first day on George
began auspiciously. True, he stopped and made as if
to gallop home shortly after leaving Jessica's; but this
was a temporary bleep. We soon fell in with other
horses, and George trotted side by side with them,
becoming steadily more alert as we approached the
meet, but standing calmly to attention when we
arrived there. I was complimented on my smart
costume, and especially on the superior quality of the
boots. As for George the general view was that he
was a good sort, made for the job, a goer if ever you

saw one, up to weight and legs like tree-trunks. And although, when I named the place where I had found him, a few eyebrows were raised, it was agreed that you could find good horses anywhere as long as you had the eye for them and by God he looked the part. In short, I trotted off from the meet aglow with pride and almost believing that my reputation as a daft professor had been finally discarded.

As soon as we left the road towards our first covert, however, George began to buck. Now there is only one reliable way to stop a horse from bucking, which is to kick him into a gallop, so stretching the legs. Instead I pulled hard on the reins, compacting George's body and increasing the size and determination of his kicks. 'Let him go!' someone shouted. The command was redundant, since by now I had fallen forward on to George's neck, which was thrashing the air like the tail of a porpoise, and the reins had slipped from my hands. A jump lay ahead, and as George flew towards it my feet slipped backwards. I was now lying horizontally along the saddle, my stirrup-less feet in the air behind me, my face pressed hard into George's plaited mane.

Nothing about horses is more beautiful or endearing than the scent of their necks – an ambrosial sweetness of malted barley and fermenting hay, lying over those throbbing muscles like a silken tunic on the thigh of Juno. To press your nose into a horse's neck is to find an instant antidote to human folly, and whenever I am in a vanity-of-vanities mood I hold my face against Sam's attentive wind-pipe and recite

Ecclesiastes, breathing deeply and twining my fingers in his mane.

This therapy requires two stationary animals, with all six feet on the ground. This was manifestly not our case on that memorable day, and although, by some miracle, I was still aloft on George when we landed beyond the rails, it was unlikely that I would stay there for long. My embarrassment was increased by the cries that preceded our take-off: 'Mind that horse!', 'Don't cut me up!' – for George had committed the cardinal sin of the hunter, which is to barge to the front at a jump. To complete the humiliation, Enoch's tightly fitting coat seemed to be letting go of my right shoulder, with a toneless tearing sound not unlike the voice of the man himself.

> Betwixt the stirrup and the ground
> Mercy I asked, mercy I found.

William Camden's epitaph for a man killed by falling from his horse rings true. The time between losing your stirrup and reaching the ground is a small eternity – a time of meditation and wonder, of sudden clarity and prayer. What to the outsider is barely a second, to the helpless sufferer contains the thought and feeling of a lifetime, and the greatest decision I ever made was in the last moment of consciousness while falling from Barney. That was later, however, when life had already changed beyond measure. My one concern as I fell from George was to avoid being trampled. I clung to the neck, but found nothing to hold. I closed my eyes as the green wall of grass approached. The ground rushed to meet me and then, with a hammer-like conviction, began to seize me and shake me like a long-lost son. George's feet skipped lightly over me, and for a second everything was still, with the uncanny stillness that precedes the moment of pain.

But the pain did not come. I got to my feet, resolved to go home and start again with my riding lessons. The man who rescued George and brought him back to me was a cheerful farmer, who told me not to be a bloody fool. What did it matter that I had fallen? What did it matter that my old coat was hanging in two segments, torn from the right shoulder to the small of the back? What did anything matter once the action had started? With weak hands and trembling legs I tried to get one foot in the stirrup. George was excited, his eyes keenly fixed on the vanishing herd, and would not stay still. Besides he was too tall, and his flanks trembled like a cliff in an earthquake. I would need a mounting block, maybe a winch or a hoist.

We found a stone wall by the road, where I could stand while my companion held George's head. No sooner was I aboard than we were off at a canter, through country which I had known by walking and cycling, but which looked entirely different between the ears of a horse – somehow more truly there, more determinedly thingish and other and with an obstinate will-less resistance of its own. These peaceful, dreamy English lanes and ditches are not what they seem: they come at you with all the speed and ferocity of the turning globe, and they come at you with teeth of stone. Borne hectically towards them, the hammering feet beneath you, your legs a-tremble in stirrups that slip and slide, you consciously feel what Heidegger says we deeply feel at all times – *geworfen*, thrown.

There were three more unavoidable jumps that day, and at each of them I fell. By the time I returned to Jessica's little remained of Enoch's coat, less of my equestrian pride, and less still of George's patience. But we had survived, and when, two months later, I was hunting on a six-mile point that lasted until dark, taking in a five-bar gate that George alone, apart from the Master and the huntsman, would jump, I remembered the farmer who had helped me back into the saddle. And I wished that someone had stood astride my life twenty years earlier, and told me, as I turned away from real decisions, not to be a bloody fool.

CHAPTER THREE

Intermezzo – The Philosophy of Hunting

Ten years have passed since those first attempts. It is
August, a sunny morning, and a light breeze ruffles
the willow-trees along the ditch. Before my window
lies the sloping pasture of Sunday Hill, once attached
to the house where I write, but now the site of a
cattle farm. The Royal Forest of Braydon, which
covered this part of England, was the favourite
hunting ground of Plantagenet kings. Scattered oaks
along the blackthorn hedgerows, and here and there
a copse of oak or ash, remind us of that royal past,
when wild boar, fallow deer and pine marten roamed
the forest glades. Now the hillside is a smooth
cushion of grass, and a herd of Friesians stands on it,
motionless in the shifting sunlight, as the scattered
flocks of cloud patrol the sky.

The hill descends to a sheltered valley, where an
ancient oak tree stands, survivor of the forest. Its
leaves and branches are dusted for me with the glow
of ownership. Here is where my life is, the place to
which I came four years ago, after three decades of
things not heard but overheard – footsteps, traffic,
street-noise, the music of unmusical neighbours – and

things not seen but registered – street-lamps, shop signs, adverts, enigmatic messages on flickering screens. Now sounds and sights hold firm before me, and those sounds and sights are mine.

I watch as a heron rises from the tangled pond beside the oak tree; two carrion crows launch themselves from the upper branches, chasing him with raucous cries over the horizon. Then all is quiet: only the distant croak of a pheasant, and the quiet murmur as the willows, stirred by the breeze, whisper the sound of their local name: *withy 'with-thee'*. Beneath the tree five horses stand in a circle, each fanning with his tail the head of his neighbour, and each resting a back leg on its metalled toe, eyes half-closed, head gently nodding. They are the reason for my being here, and I study them with interest and pride.

Work has not gone well. I am trying to write a lecture – the Sir Leslie Stephen Memorial Lecture, for Cambridge University. I am not up to the job; for one thing, I am no longer an academic – since discovering hunting, my priorities have changed. Besides, there is hardly a subject on which I could address a crowd of undergraduates, certainly no subject relevant to the life and thought of Sir Leslie Stephen. I respect Sir Leslie, who set a standard for literary criticism that everyone should follow, and who created, in *The Dictionary of National Biography*, a monument to our national culture as great as any built in stone. I revere him too as the brother of Sir James Fitzjames Stephen – the great Indian judge whose cantankerous philosophy I endorse entirely. But about his children I have mixed feelings, and especially about Virginia Woolf. It was Woolf and her kind who did most to locate the heart of modern England in the same place as its head – namely, in colleges and drawing rooms. Great writer though she was, Woolf was part of the revenge that modern England took on its past – the revenge of an educated class which has lost its attachment to the land and begun to dance to the rhythms of the city. Perhaps it is only the French who understand cities. English art, English music and English literature seem to become spindly, arcane and ephemeral, just as soon as they are translated from their rural context. Among Englishmen only Dickens wrote well of city life – but he wrote of it as something monstrous, alien and demonic.

A theme for the lecture? Not really. Too vast and vague and volatile; and too distant from the thoughts of modern youth.

My eyes return to the oak tree. Sam, the big black gelding, whom I should describe as 'brown' since that is the word applied to black horses, though maybe this raises an issue of political correctness – Sam has turned round to face Barney, the liver chestnut who is captain of the herd. The two horses rise on their hind legs and playfully box with their hooves, tossing their manes in a display of masculine rivalry. They have sniffed it in the wind – the first breath of autumn, the smell of ripening berries and stubble fields. Each day since exercise began they have been more alert, their ears pricked to distant sounds, their nostrils flaring. Now they know. Hunting is about to begin.

Horses are creatures of habit. Provide them with a genial routine and they will be content. But this does not mean that the quality of their life is everywhere the same. On the contrary. Only one kind of horse gets the most out of being a horse and that is the hunter. Alone among domesticated animals the hunter has the chance to run with the herd – fit, well-fed and carefree – over country cleared of his natural predators. No equine joy matches that of running side by side with other horses, immersed in the great tide of species-life and excited by the baying of hounds – a sound that stirs a collective memory of primeval terror, but which echoes back from those unconscious reaches not as terror but as joy. The horse became the remarkable thing that he is by fleeing that sound. He finds his fulfilment in pursuing it.

Something similar is true of us. We began as prey, saved ourselves by preying and acquired meanwhile a blood-filling joy in the chase. And our success in both hunting and battle was brought about, first by our ability to co-operate with each other, secondly by our ability to co-operate with horses. The extraordinary accident of nature, which enabled man and horse to meld into a centaur, may even be responsible for the survival of both our species.* Like the horse, man is

* I am trying to avoid references; but *The Nature of Horses,* by

a social animal, who survives as a group or not at all. Like the horse, he faces danger and hardship collectively. And like the horse, he saves himself by a common feat of exertion. All these ancient and once much-visited truths are stirred in the moment of hunting, and come vividly alive in us as we return, together with our two most trusted friends among the animals, to the primordial thrill of contest.

The subject for a lecture? Not really. My generation of grammar school-boys enjoyed an influx of wonderful teachers: Oxbridge graduates who had gone with missionary zeal to the colonies, to return with a vision of their homeland and an urgent desire to impart that vision to the young. We were raised on Virgil, Homer and Shakespeare; we were introduced to the repertoire of classical music, and knew the rhythm of the hunt from Schumann and Berlioz; we read the great works of anthropology – Frazer's *Golden Bough*, Malinowski's *Sex and Repression in Savage Society*, Ruth Benedict's *Patterns of Culture*. And most of us had encountered *Moby-Dick*, and heard in that rolling, seething, oceanic prose the far-off exultant cry of man the species.

With such a background a teacher could perhaps make a start on conveying these difficult matters – and nothing is more difficult to convey than a joy that you do not know at first hand. But now? From

Stephen Budiansky (Weidenfeld, London, 1997) covers the ground so well that I will be forgiven by anybody who has time to look up this source.

what frame of reference do you begin, when addressing post-modern students?

I turn back to my desk. This year's Stephen lecture
will be about pop music. Sam and Barney have set off
at a gallop, the other horses starting up and after
them, the field a trembling drum-skin under their
hooves: how different from Oasis or The Verve, this
natural rhythm of excited animals. People often
criticize pop as animal noises; but that's because they
don't know much about animals, or much about
noise. There is nothing animal in Oasis. The sparse
melodic lines and unbroken rhythms are by-products
of the machine – the man-made measure that ticks in
the background of modern life, eliding every pause
and effacing every silence. What passes for life in this
music is not life at all, but a repetitious discharge, a
monotonous spasm like the jerk of a frog's leg wired
to the mains.

No chance of persuading them of that. For only the
person who knows music other than pop will have
the faintest idea what I mean by 'life' – the life that
drives the 'Jupiter' to its inevitable ending, or which
breathes softly and rhythmically in a Schubert song.
Modern people are losing contact with life – both
with its artistic image, and with the thing itself, that
outgoing innocent love of being that I hear in
Barney's hooves and which has been banished from
Oasis as it has been banished from the condition to
which their music ministers. In an age of the machine
the rhythms of life are beaten down by hammer

blows and driven into the unconscious, where they
dwindle and die.

Unless, that is, you rewaken them. And there are
two things that reawaken them in me: dancing (by
which I mean the old-fashioned activity which occurs
between consenting adults in public), and hunting.
Other people have other methods. But these are my
tonic, and hunting the dearest. For hunting lifts me
out of my modernist solitude and throws me down in
a pre-modern herd – a composite herd, made up of
horse and hound and human, each sharing its gift of
excitement and giving its all to the chase.

The ancient and venerable character of hunting is
essential to its atmosphere. For millions of years we
were at one with the animals, hunting and hunted by
turns. The tribe lifted itself from the natural world,
to become civilized, law-governed and political. In
retrospect, this was sheer madness. But the tribal
divinities authorized our reckless gesture. Hunting
became a ceremony, an act of worship, in which the
old forces, embodied in the totem, were pursued and
captured and their forgiveness implored. As he
hunted with his fellows, the tribesman felt absolution
in the blood. Exposed to collective danger, he showed
to the animals that he still belonged with them, that
his civilized apart-ness was earned through courage
and skill. And the more civilized man became, the
more necessary was this act of penitence. That is why
'field sports' have been the recreation of aristocrats.
Those with the highest civilization are most in need
of forgiveness for it. Today we are all civilized –

which is to say that we have all left the fold of nature and live from the funds of human artifice. But, unlike the old aristocracy, we lack culture, and therefore lack the ready awareness of our condition. We live in a virtual world. TV, computer screens and the simmering background of comforts create an illusion of well-being with the bare minimum of physical and spiritual exertion. Our remoteness from the natural order is ever increasing. And our awareness of what this means is ever less.

In those centaur hours, however, real life returns to you. For a brief ecstatic moment the blood of another species flows through your veins, stirring the old deposits of collective life, releasing pockets of energy that a million generations laboriously harvested from the crop of human suffering. And this intimate union between species transfers to our human mind not the excitement of the animals only, but also the innocent concreteness of their thoughts.

Since taking up hunting, I have often reflected on Heidegger, the nature-loving philosopher who coated concrete things with abstract words, like a confectioner smearing cakes with chocolate. Admittedly, he was no great advert for philosophy, hiding from his guilt in the forest, pretending to be a child of nature in a peasant's smock, and not seeing the trees for the wood. But he made concrete reality enticing, by dressing it as something abstract – mysterious as those chocolate-coated cakes. And in one thing he was right. We misunderstand the world if we see it only through concepts: divided, sorted, stacked up, explained. The Being of things is a being-to-hand: we know things by using them.

The very life of an animal is a being-to-hand, a using which is also a being-used. But did Heidegger experience, I wonder, the upward thrust of a horse's hoof as it impacts through the saddle? Probably not. Through his swaying, abstract sentences, burdened like unmilked cows and mooing piteously at the gate of sense, the ground is barely visible. Of course, there are those famous essays: on Van Gogh's boots, on Hölderlin's mystical homecoming, on building and dwelling. But even this thinker, who made soil and ground and rootedness into icons of our human state, gives no true living sense of trodden earth – the earth which Barney consumes with his strides, taking in with an intelligence that always surprises me, the minute map of holes and ditches which unwinds like a cine-reel before his speeding muzzle.

Abstract thinkers must renew their awareness of the really real. They should hunger for the sight and smell and touch of things, and nothing brings the sensuous reality into focus more clearly than hunting. This 'Being' that Heidegger refers to, as though it were some glutinous stuff from which the little shoots of '*Dasein*' (you and me) sprout up like curious protozoa – what has it to do with the spring of turf, the ooze of river bank and the muddy grind of gravel in which this sure believing hoof is planted? The ground is not one but many – hard and soft, sharp and yielding, dry and wet, grass-canopied or raw beneath the scattered rout of last year's vegetation.

Pad, hoof and foot follow in turn through this multifaceted terrain, grasping it as an infant grasps its mother, knowing the taste and touch of every part. And aloft among these flying animals you re-enter the state which our ancestors renounced for comfort's sake, the state in which the nearness of death compels you to humility.

The horses pull up short and prick their ears. I go to the window and listen. A lorry is reversing in the farm next door, and the little warning noise it makes is like the horn of the huntsman sounding from afar. Soon they understand, and quietly, with that easy resumption of routine which is the blessing of herds, they return to their grazing. And I return, less easily, to my singular and solitary task.

In one respect pop music is like hunting. For both involve survivals of totemism. The fan is bound to his favourite group less by the music than by a bond of membership. The singer is a totem, the everlasting symbol of the tribe. He is iconized, endowed with a more than human presence. He may, like Elvis, survive death in a thousand look-alikes and sing-alikes. And if he is not careful, he will suffer the fate of other totem animals, and be ritually destroyed by the Bacchantes that dog his steps, shot like John Lennon in a frenzy of self-inflicted grief. The difference between this kind of totemism and that of the hunter casts light on the great divide between town and country. Pop culture springs from the tribal life of towns. The adolescents who cluster around their idol are arrested in a posture of

transgression. Nothing in their experience conducts
them from the intoxicated dream of youth into the
sober reality of parenthood. Theirs is a tribal life, but
one with no rite of passage.

The community of hunters is quite different. It
retains the courtesies and formalities of a disciplined
endeavour, and with them its rites of passage. The
hunt is a society which you join by degrees, which
involves ceremonies of initiation, a radical distinction
between those who are already trusted and those who
will be in time, and between the children, the youth,
the braves and the elders. Even now a child may be
'blooded' with the wounds of the totem – a barbarous
practice, say some, but one which engages with the
most vital of human needs, the need for a social
membership that goes deeper than chatter and deeper
than choice.

How easy it is to write about something – even
about pop music – when it is approached in this
Darwinian frame of mind. I sketch out the lecture and
return in my thoughts to hunting.

I incline to Schiller's view, that the most serious
things in life are without a purpose, like art, poetry
and music, like friendship, sport and play. Play is the
child's prerogative; the adult, if he is not to play for
ever, needs other and more demanding recreations.
His sense of responsibility and communal risk must
be activated if he is to become what he truly is. And
that is why hunting is good for us.

Deep down in all of us there are psychic residues,
inherited from our hunter-gatherer ancestors, which

speak to us of another and simpler world. It was a world in which we were at home, since we were adapted to it by evolution. Our instincts, our spontaneous perceptions, movements and social feelings, bear witness to that distant and never-to-be-recovered condition in which the separation of man from nature had yet to occur. And the strain of modern life would be unbearable, if we did not rehearse the spontaneous psychic movements that were implanted by the species, and which are as important for our proper functioning as it is important to a dog that he should bark from time to time, or to a chicken that she should lay an egg. This is the truth in those myths of Paradise and Fall, which have brought so much consolation to our species. Planted in us, too deep for memory, are the instincts of the hunter-gatherer, who differs from his civilized descendants not only in making no distinction between the natural and the artificial order, but also in relating to his own and other species in a herd-like way.

The hunter-gatherer is a spontaneous 'joiner', who co-operates not only with his own species, but also with those that are most readily adapted to his hunting: with horse, hound, falcon and ferret. Towards his prey he takes a quasi-religious attitude. The hunted animal is hunted as an individual. But the hunted species is elevated to divine status as the totem, and a kind of mystical union of the tribe with its totem seals the pact between them for ever.

At the universal level, the hunter-gatherer *is* the tribe, which *is* the deer or antelope, conceived as a

species. This mystical thought guides the hunter in
the field. The experience of the hunter involves a
union of opposites – absolute antagonism between
individuals resolved through a mystical identity of
species. By pursuing the individual, and worshipping
the species, the hunter guarantees the eternal recurrence of his prey. Hence the words which R. S.
Surtees puts into the mouth of his imagined cockney
huntsman, Jorrocks: '...my affection for him is a
perfect paradox. In the summer I loves him with all
the hardour of affection: not an 'air of his beautiful
'ead would I 'urt; the sight of him is more glorious
than the Lord Mayor's show, but when the autumn
comes then dash my vig how I loves to pursue him to
destruction.' One hundred and fifty years ago there
appeared *The Life of a Fox, written by himself* – a
humane but unsentimental account of the life and
fears and comforts of the vulpine species, informed by
a deep sympathy for the fox and an abhorrence of
human cruelty. Its author was Thomas Smith,
huntsman of the Pytchley, and one notorious for his
relentless antagonism towards his quarry, once in the
field.

We relate to one another as individuals, and the
soul is the animating principle which makes a person
who he is. In the case of human beings, therefore, the
soul is the self. In the case of wild animals, to which
we relate as interchangeable members of their species, the soul-idea becomes attached to the species. In
Ovid's *Metamorphoses* the stories are told of the
halcyon and the nightingale, who embody in their

species-being a soul which, in human shape, had been the soul of an individual. The idea of the species-soul is still with us. For the fisherman the individual trout on his line is also The Trout, the universal whose soul he knows in many instances, and which he loves with the greater passion in the moment when he pits himself against the mere individual who is its passing incarnation. This attitude is exalted by totemism into a religious idea: the universal species becomes a sacred object, to which the particular quarry is a sacrifice. The quarry dies on behalf of the species, and thereby re-consecrates the identity between species and tribe.

This way of relating to animals is less familiar to those who know only pets. For domestic animals have a kind of personality bestowed by our daily dealings. We treat them as individuals and they learn to respond as such. The hunter-gatherer, in his original condition, has little room for such an attitude. In time, however, he learns to enhance his powers by co-operating with other species – and in particular with hound and horse. The history of this process has been recorded only in its later stages – by Xenophon, for example, in his *Cynergeticus*, which remains one of the most penetrating works on the art of hunting with hounds. Nevertheless, it is the beginning of a new relation to the natural world: the relation which stems from our role as a dominant species, able to conscript other species to our purposes, and to exploit their instincts.

The hunter now works side by side with animals whom he treats as individuals, in hot pursuit of the prey whose individuality is lent to it only temporarily, as it were, and because it has been singled out by the chase. The horse beneath him is Sam or Barney, whose habits he knows, and with whom he communicates directly; the hounds to whom he calls are Saviour, Sanguine and Sonorous, and he addresses them by name, aware of their individual virtues and vices, for which he makes constant allowance. But the fox – the generic being who appears equally in Aesop and Surtees, in La Fontaine and Stravinsky, and who still retains his totemic names of Reynard and Charlie* – is merely incarnate in the hunted animal and will survive its death. For the brief moment of the chase, Charlie is an individual, to be understood through the beliefs and strategies, the vulpine strengths and weaknesses that distinguish this particular instance. Once killed, however, he returns to his archetypal condition, reassuming his nature as The Fox, whom the huntsman knows and loves, and whose eternal recurrence is his deep desire.

Thus it is that the huntsman who has shot the cunning little vixen in Janáček's beautiful opera also rejoices to rediscover her in the vixen's daughter. And this rediscovery is not of the individual vixen,

---

* This name has been recently acquired, from Charles James Fox, the eighteenth-century Whig. It was inspiring to the landowning classes, during the ardours of the chase, to imagine their enemy in front of them.

but of the universal Vixen, and of the natural context which provides her life.

This return to a previous relation with the natural world is now rare. But we should try to understand the longings and frustrations of those who seek for it. In the civilized world, where food is not hunted or gathered but produced, hunting and gathering become forms of recreation. But they awaken the old instincts and desires, the old pieties and the old relations with our own and other species. If your purpose in angling is to catch a fish, then how simply this could be achieved with an electrode, which stuns the population of the river, and brings it unconscious to the surface. But what angler would look on this method with favour? To catch fish in this way is to cross the barrier between the natural and the artificial – it is to conquer another portion of nature for the world of machinery. Yet the point of angling was to return, in however well-protected a guise, to the natural world, the world unblemished by our footsteps.

If we think in that way, then we can hardly avoid the conclusion that totemic attitudes have been planted in us by evolution. But ought we to think in that way? The question often occupies me as we move from covert to covert, on those afternoons when scent is poor or foxes scarce.

Here is what I have come to think. We have evolved in the same way and under the same pressures as other animals. Our physical nature, our aptitudes, our repertoire of movement, appetite and behaviour can all be explained (up to a point) in evolutionary terms. But, however far we take the explanation, it gives us at best only one half of the picture. It is describing the human object, but not the human subject. When I look at you and see you smile, I see the jaw and lips which contort themselves in response to nervous impulses from the brain; but I also see the person who smiles, and whose freedom is revealed in his smiling. The relation between object and subject is like that between the pigments on a canvas and the face that we perceive in them. Science describes and explains the pigments; but it makes no mention of the painted saint. In the same way, the human soul, its freedom, translucency and moral presence are never mentioned in the book of evolution. They are there for us to perceive, when we look at the world from 'I' to 'I', but science overlooks them.

Science has its proselytizers and tub-thumpers – people who tell us that God is now redundant, and should be peaceably or forcibly retired. The smallest dose of philosophy would cure mankind of this delusion. All that science can show us is the *how* of God's creation; never can we by scientific means disprove the *fact* of it, still less cast light on the *why*. But the answer to the *why* lies here and now, in you and me – in the free and reflective being which is *Dasein*, but which, had Heidegger been less in thrall to the German language, he might have called *Hiersein* – being here. 'Be here now!' says Oasis. Fine, if you acknowledge the cost. To live properly in the present tense you must be conscious of the past and future. And to be fully *here* you must be joined to others in a web of moral concern.

God intended that we live in such a way, that we see into the subjectivity of one another, and into the subjectivity of the world – which is God himself. That we can do this is self-evident. How we do it is an unfathomable mystery. And if, in order to bring this mystery about, a process of evolution was required, so that the soul became incarnate at last in a creature which rose only by degrees to such an eminence, then so be it. God moves in a mysterious way. When you look on people as objects, then you see that Darwin was right. When you look on them as subjects, you see that the most important thing about them has no place in Darwin's theory.

And animals? Either they are pets – honorary subjects, who borrow a soul from those who love them – or they are wild, adrift in the natural order, part of the great bruised organism which is threatened by our human arrogance. To relate to animals as wild things we must see them as we see nature when the divine idea shines through to us. Rarely does this happen. But it can happen all the same, and is never more likely to happen than when hunting amid the herd and the pack, on the lively scent of a fox who streams through the hedgerows, staking out the landscape with a matrix of primeval desire.

CHAPTER FOUR

Middle

The significance of a human experience can be measured by the quantity and quality of its art. By this criterion religion and erotic love are the deepest of our poor resources; but hunting, however distant on the surface, lies adjacent to them in the depths. What else explains the mysterious and soul-shaking chemistry that Wagner works in the second act of *Tristan*, as Isolde sings out her impatient love above the distant sound of hunting? Listen carefully to this passage, and you will hear something that cannot be put into words, but which lies as deep in you as it does in me.

It is to hunting with hounds, and the unique love that grows through it, that Homer owes his most beautifully understated stroke of drama — the moment of Odysseus's return in disguise to Ithaca, when he is recognized by his favourite hound Argos, who lies dying on the muck-heap. The dog flattens his ears and wags his tail, too weak now for other greeting. And the hero, before departing on his urgent business, wipes away a furtive tear. 'As for Argos, the fate of black death seized him straightway

when he had seen Odysseus in the twentieth year'.
(*Odyssey* 17, 326–7.)

Homer's epics were the first and greatest in our
literature. The theme of hunting has run through all
the epics that followed; it has formed the background
to Medieval poetry, surged and resurged in seven-
teenth-century drama, constantly broken the flow of
eighteenth-century novels, and finally achieved a
great epic of its own, in Herman Melville's *Moby-
Dick*, a work steeped in the awe, fear, love and pity
which the animal kingdom stirs in us. And although
organized fox-hunting of the kind we know today
came comparatively late on the scene, no sooner was
it with us than it spawned a literature as original and
curious as any in the libraries of the world.

The first extended example of this literature is a
poem in blank verse by William Somerville, called
The Chase, published in 1735, shortly after James
Thomson's *Seasons*, the diction and rhythms of which
it imitates. Somerville dealt with hare- and stag-
hunting, as well as fox-hunting, and provided a
learned and accurate manual for the practitioner. He
also gave the description of hunting which has
always been most popular among its adepts:

> the sport of kings,
> Image of war without the danger.

Surtees corrected this to 'the sport of kings, the
image of war without its guilt, and only five-and-

twenty per cent. of its danger,' which is the cockney grocer's version of the same chivalrous idea.

It was Fielding, however, who really launched fox-hunting as a literary theme, perceiving in it a wonderful foil for eccentricity, and a way to build character without advancing the plot. Squire Western is the first of many portraits of country types, whose Englishness is of a piece with their willingness to break their necks at a gate or a bullfinch. During the nineteenth century the hunting field was a place where social classes mixed, subjecting themselves to a common danger and recognizing, if only for a moment, a common fragility and a common need for help. Fox-hunting provided the opportunity to study the new forms of lunacy which the rising classes were bringing to country life, so replenishing the dwindling stock of lunacy bequeathed by the landed gentry.

If you wish to know what fox-hunting is, and why it is beyond measure beautiful and compelling and obsessing, then you should read the novels of R. S. Surtees – *Handley Cross*, and *Mr Sponge's Sporting Tour* – novels which do not merely capture the deep emotions that focus on this sport, but provide an inimitable record of the society that grew around it in the nineteenth century. In Surtees' cockney hero – the shopkeeper, John Jorrocks, MFH, who sells tea to the gentry while jumping beside them over hedges – we see one vivid stage in the process which has been completed in our day: the transition of the countryside from a place of feudal labour to one of retirement for the middle class. Kipling reproved the novelist for his 'ill-considered spawn of Dickens and horse-dung characters'. But this is scarcely fair, since the influence runs from Surtees to Dickens and not the other way.

Nor should you neglect the brilliant descriptions of the chase in Trollope and Siegfried Sassoon, the evocations of particular hunts and particular characters contained in the sporting journalism of C. J. Apperley ('Nimrod'), the novels of G. J. Whyte-Melville, or the stories of Somerville and Ross, those Irish ladies who sublimated their Sapphic love in pithy images of a life among horses and hounds. Even Virginia Woolf, so remote from them in thought and style, finds praise for the exponents of this peculiar literary tradition: 'In their slapdash, gentlemanly way they have ridden their pens as boldly as they have ridden their horses. They have had their effect upon the language. This riding and tumbling, this being blown upon and rained upon and splashed from head to heels with mud, have worked themselves into the very texture of English prose and given it that leap and dash, that stripping of images from flying hedge and tossing tree which distinguish it not indeed above the French but so emphatically from it.'

It is not only the thrill and danger of the chase that appeals to those who have re-created it in literature. Hunting awakens a lively and unsentimental sympathy for animals, of a kind unknown to the lover of pets. There is perhaps no greater evocation of pity for a stricken creature than the eighty-first chapter of

Melville's glowing masterpiece, nor is there a more
succinct description of a fox's despair than that in *Sir
Gawain and the Green Knight*:

> With alle þe wo on lyue
> To þe wod he went away

With all the woe in life, the fox turned back to the
wood – the wood in which the hounds, he knew, were
after him. And in the same work (perhaps the earliest
description of a fox-hunt in English), the poet
describes the thrilling voices of hounds, the moment
of triumph, and the great surge of love between
hound and huntsman that follows.

This love between man and dog is the heart of fox-
hunting, and one of the reasons why hunting with
hounds has been so often on the tip of the poet's
tongue, and so often exalted in paint or marble or
music. It is a refreshing love, based in realistic
perceptions and mutual utility, and culminating in a
common triumph. The love that people feel for their
pets may be real, but it is seldom realistic. It rarely
occurs to the suburban dog-lover that the ease with
which his pet's affection is purchased is a sign of its
moral worthlessness. Fido's wagging tail is misread
as an endorsement, a sign that Fido has peered into
his provider's heart and been moved by the spectacle
of human kindness. The daily bowl of gravy-smeared
chunks is a reward for moral insight. As for the
creatures whose remnants lie in the bowl, the dog-
lover has no qualms about their slaughter, so long as

he does not witness it. For is it not obvious that they died to feed a moral being, a creature like you or me, whose wisdom, rationality and goodness of heart are all definitively proven by his choice of master?

No such sentiments pollute the heart of the huntsman. His hounds live still in their savage state, relieved of that constant and inachievable demand to mimic the manners of a moral being, which troubles the life of the incarcerated pet. They sleep in a pack in dog-scented kennels, hunt in a pack with their powers supremely stretched; they eat raw flesh, and not too much of it; they drink the brackish water of mud-stopped ditches; and the price of every slackness is the rough end of the tongue. Once trained to hunt they can never be subdued to a household regime, and can expect nothing when their hunting strength has gone besides a shot in the head, often administered by the very man whose love is all to them. But their time on earth is a happy one; everything they do is rooted in their nature, and even the crowning gift of human love comes in the guise of species-life: for the huntsman is leader of the pack, first among the band of canine warriors. His authority is not that mysterious, guilt-ridden thing that appears to the pet in the down-turned milky eyes of his crooning captor, but the glad imperative of the species, miraculously incarnate in human form.

For those who truly love hunting, therefore, the work of the hounds is a central part of their delight. Of course, the thrill of the chase is also important. But it is a thrill of the same kind: it comes from

sharing in the animal excitement, so that the currents
of emotion which flow from hound to horse and back
again are diverted through your pumping arteries,
dissolving human knowledge and spreading it to the
centaur limbs below.

And here we touch on the essence of sport in all its
forms. Just as there is nothing more boring than
boredom, nothing more exciting than excitement,
nothing more loveable than love or hateful than
hatred, so is there nothing that arouses interest so
much as interest. Interesting people are interested
people, and an enthusiasm – be it as thankless as
birdwatching or as bizarre as philately – marks out
the enthusiast as a source of curious learning and a
person with a mind that glows. A horse with pricked
ears and prancing steps awakens our attention; our
eyes turn in the direction to which he points his head,
and our body quickens to his ready tempo. A cat
stalking its prey in the grass, eyes wide, paw raised
and tail angrily flicking, raises the spirits like a glass
of champagne. And the highest form of animal
interest is the collective interest of the pack – the
interest that inhabits not one animal only, nor each
animal separately, but the organism which contains
them and which responds as one to the common need
of all. This is why teams are so much more gripping
than solo performers, and why the quiet absorption of
the Wimbledon stalls bears no comparison to the
riotous exultation of a Wembley football match. In
watching a team you are confronting interest that
feeds on interest, response that answers response,

perception arousing perception, as the players tremble on the unseen web of nerves that joins them.

So it is with a pack of hounds. After a few years of hunting, when I had been awarded my buttons, I would sometimes (though not often) be sent out on point. In order to understand what a privilege this is, you must take note of the greatest enemy of country life: not the car but the television. Thanks to TV modern people have lost the habit of dialogue, in which serious matters are treated in measured words; hence they have also lost the habit of silence. And it is a law of human nature that those with least to say spend the most time in saying it. Hence the hunting field abounds in foolish chatter. To some extent this has always been so. Peter Beckford, cousin of the famous eccentric of Fonthill Abbey, and author of the standard text on fox-hunting, wrote thus, two hundred years ago:

Among the ancients, it was reckoned *an ill omen* to speak in hunting: I wish it were thought so now. *Hoc age*, should be one of the first maxims in hunting, as in life: and I can assure you, when I am in the field I never wish to hear any other tongue than that of a hound.

When on point you escape to a world in which Beckford's ideal is realized, a world where every sound belongs to hunting. Deep within the scrub the hounds are at work, and for long moments you hear only the swishing of their tails in bracken, or the

cracking of the mossy twigs beneath their pads. If
the huntsman utters a sound, it is a signal sent from
beast to beast: 'Pack-hey!', 'Boyup!', 'Tikkah!' or some
such visceral noise thrown up from regions deeper
than the reach of human grammar. And as you stare
into the tangled, wintry, leafless copse, the scene
becomes subdued and still and preluding. Nature
stands before you as something not observed but
watched. The silver wrapping of a birch tree, when
the pointed muzzle of a seeking hound is pressed to
it, seems peculiarly soft and gift-like; the berries of
black bryony which hang across a hollow where the
fox might lurk are as bright and red as a painting; the
pile of golden crabs whose fermenting fumes might
foil the scent seem heaped and rich; and the fronds of
old-man's beard when lightly and vaguely shaken by
the motion underneath them of a rabbit are detached
and fleeting like an afterthought. And then, when a
startled roebuck comes bounding through the undergrowth, swerving the saplings of dogwood and
whitebeam, you notice the varying force with which
each branch resists him, and the shrubs spring back
from his passage with the same full-muscled thrust
that pushes them apart. For a moment the copse
moves with the roebuck's motion, and you irresistibly
see these things – trees and thorns and bracken,
muddy hollows, dry beds of leaf-mould and the
pulling, tearing fronds of briar – with the eyes of a
creature for whom they are both home and danger,
comfort and the enemy's disguise. The roebuck leaves

the wood, goes bouncing away, and a tense and
wakeful stillness drowns his traces.

An excited squeak rings out from the dense
interior, and all at once the web of nerves draws
tight. The hounds converge as though pulled by a
single force from every corner. Soon the covert rings
with their cries, the huntsman's horn is stuttering
encouragement, and the crash of a horse in the
undergrowth betrays the whipper-in – that indispen-
sable servant of the huntsman, who keeps the hounds
together and stops them from 'rioting' after forbidden
prey. The copse echoes to the choir of hounds like the
vault of some great cathedral:

> ... besides the groves,
> The skies, the fountains, every region near
> Seem'd all one mutual cry: I never heard
> So musical a discord, such sweet thunder.

So Hippolyta describes the sound in *A Midsummer
Night's Dream*. And while it must be the most
dreadful of war-cries in the ear of the fox, the rest of
nature seems to respond in sympathy. The birds fall
into a listening silence, and your horse begins to shift
and shiver beneath you, awaiting with excitement the
chase that must soon begin.

Then, just as suddenly, the commotion ceases and
everything goes dead. An air of stagnant puzzlement
hangs over the scene. Now it is not the springy
saplings which capture your eye, but the older, wiser

and more gloomy trees, the oaks and ashes and
sycamores which stand unmoved in the pond of
silence, the sap frozen in their veins, the life
withdrawn from them. Nothing stirs or speaks, and
the huntsman is purposefully still within the covert,
keeping counsel as the hydra-headed pack of hounds
ponders the vanished scent. Has he gone to ground?
Is he lying low? Was it a 'heel line'? Did he jump
aside or double back? Such questions are not explicit
in the canine mind as they are in ours. But their force
is all the greater for being buried, and they pass from
hound to hound through unseen catacombs of
species-life. The intensity of concentration in the
wood is palpable; for a moment even the trees have a
thinking, frowning look.

And then, if you are lucky, you will see him,
creeping on his belly without a sound along the
covert's edge, looking for the place where he can
break with the best of chances. In some languages 'to
be silent' is rendered by an active verb – *schweigen* in
German, *mlčet* in Czech. True silence is a creative
doing, an intent and strenuous exercise of mind and
body, matching, in this moment, the concentrated
labour of the fox. And as you watch his alert and
careful movements he may suddenly turn and fix you
with his white mask, taking in the man on horseback
watching him, and then slinking further off, in the
hope of breaking covert unobserved.

The hunted fox, when fresh, has an aura which
cannot be captured in words, nor even in pictures.

Grantley Berkeley, huntsman and Member of Parliament, whose *Reminiscences of a Huntsman* appeared in 1854, wrote thus:

> A fox has ... a large amount of reasoning faculty in his beautiful head, the very expression of his eye tells it, and it is further proved by the impossibility of the stuffer or preserver of beasts and birds to give the specimen its crafty and observant expression; it is also beyond the power of the painter.

It is beyond the power of the photographer too. For this intense and knowing expression is read in the fox's mask only by those who are hunting him, and who are caught in the electric thrill of contest. Here is the origin of that universal impulse of hunter-gatherers, to invest their quarry with a human soul. Nothing less than this will meet the need of the moment, and it is nature's need, not yours.

The fox breaks covert at last, a halloa sounds, and after the brief minute needed to converge on a common exit, the pack appears in the open, pouring like troopers from a trench and fanning out along the edge of the wood until one of them lights on the scent and sends up a cry of triumph. Now the chase begins, with the fox well ahead, crossing hedges where he can, since hounds must climb and push against the thorn matting, while he runs quickly through. If he sees a field of sheep he will make for it: sheep-stain foils a fox's scent as effectively as Muzak cancels thought. Often you can tell from afar where the fox is running, by watching the movements of sheep, who will break asunder to let him pass, remembering those days as lambs when he was their deadly enemy. Sometimes his passage through a wood is betrayed by birds – for the jay, the magpie and the blackbird will chatter their alarms at passing foxes, and carrion crows may sometimes mob a fox from field to field.

Hounds are most beautiful when hunting on a line – each speaking to the scent, and trusting both himself and the one who gallops just ahead of him. But because the hound has poor vision, he depends upon the scent to find his quarry, and the scent may be spoiled or scattered; it may hang in patches or be blown by the wind. Indeed, there is no medium for conveying information that is more vacillating than scent; nor is there a huntsman who can tell you which conditions are good for scenting, and which conditions bad. All that the huntsman knows is that the hounds rely on him when the scent runs cold. Without him, they will feather away from the line and lose their collective momentum. The huntsman, as Grantley Berkeley puts it, must be able to 'guess a fox to death'. When the hounds have come to a 'check' they 'throw up' – that is, they stand and stare with their heads held high. The huntsman must gather them together and 'cast' them to a place where the scent will revive, or from where, by moving in a pattern, they will re-discover it. How a huntsman does this, with what information and by what instinctive knowledge of the fox's flight, is a mystery beyond human telling, although many a huntsman

has tried without success to convey it. And one of the
reasons for following on horseback, and doing your
best to stay in touch, is that you will time and again
perceive this momentous episode, in which the all-
but-sufficient information contained in a canine
collective is suddenly completed by a human
thought, and expressed with cries of exultation as the
noses turn once more the fox's traces. It is at the
moment of the cast that the mysterious inner identity
between huntsman and hounds becomes apparent –
an identity which for ever sunders the huntsman
from the rest of human kind. He is the Green Knight,
the forest's revenge, the wild thing on life's horizon,
whom we glimpse in the *Schöne Müllerin* of Schubert,
and who secretly bays at the moon.

But of course there are other reasons for following
on horseback. The horse's interest multiplies tenfold
the interest of his rider. Once the hounds are in the
covert, the experienced hunter will prick his ears and
stare into the wood, following every sound and
movement, sensing that he soon must run. He will
often know before you do that the hounds have left
covert on the other side, and when he has caught
sight of them, he will watch their movement carefully
taking his measure of the land ahead. Then there is
the chase – which need be neither wild nor fast nor
dangerous, but which, in its steadiness and determination, passes back to you through equine limbs the
dire resolution of the fox. Each obstacle before you is
one that *he* has taken, each stream a stream that *he*
has crossed, each copse or wooded path a place where

he has vainly sought to save himself. Only on
horseback do you obtain the full measure of his speed
and cunning, and although the huntsman must do his
best to kill his quarry — for this is the goal on which
all else depends — there is scarcely a mounted
follower who is glad of the death or unmoved to
sympathy with the creature whose arduous course he
has himself so arduously followed.

The mounted follower is also brought nearer to his
kind, by enjoying their hospitality. Culture came
when wandering ceased, when the land was settled
and parcelled out, and the people learned to stay put
amid their crops and animals. In Jack Scruton's view
the land should still be common land, and all its
produce shared. But this would reduce the fields to
infertile scrub; it would remove the coverts and
spinneys and hedgerows which came with the enclo-
sures; it would destroy the primary cause of those
stone barns and timbered cottages which were, for
my father, the symbol of a life worth living, because
lived from generation to generation in a single place.
Marx writes of enclosure as the original sin, which
cast man out from the natural world. Should we not
say, rather, that it was the first step towards that
higher nature which comes through owning and
giving? At any rate, enclosure was no ordinary fault,
but the *felix culpa* which gave to the landscape its
human face. Crossing the country on a hunting day
you are the guest of private owners, and the land
beneath your horse's feet is a place of dwelling.

Hospitality is the price paid for the social acceptance of private wealth. Ownership of land is particularly sensitive, since it places tangible obstacles in the
way of those who do not enjoy it, and restricts the
supply of every raw material. The farmer who forbids
the rambler is very likely to permit the hunt,
regardless of whether he is plagued by foxes, and
notwithstanding the fact that the hunt does far more
damage than a quiet walker in an anorak. For the
rambler is an 'off-comer', someone who does not
'belong'. The farmer needs to justify his ownership to
his neighbours, to those with whom he lives as one
possessor among others. Hospitality extends to them,
since they enjoy the same ancestral title to the
territory from which his portion has been carved.
Hence, when the hunt meets on his land, the farmer
will offer stirrup cups and sausages, in order to
confirm that the land is open to his guests.

Ceremonial hospitality of this kind is not like
ordinary giving. It is an attempt to raise the relations
among neighbours to a higher level: to confer
legitimacy and permanence on the current patterns of
ownership. It is partly in acknowledgement of this
that mounted followers wear a uniform. The hunt
arrives on the farmer's land not as an ordinary
visitor, but as a travelling festival, endorsing his
ownership in the act of exploiting it.

And finally there is the weather. Although frozen
ground, which would lame both hound and horse,
brings hunting to a stop, all other weathers feed the
joy of it. You might be hacking off on a crisp

December morning, with the pale winter sun spar-
kling in the hoar-frost along the hedgerows, and
playing on the polished forms of horses as they
appear on every hilltop, converging on the meet. You
might be hunting on a blustery day in February,
when suddenly the blood-red clotting sun drops into
the slit of the far horizon, and the grass is criss-
crossed with golden fibres like a weaver's loom,
becoming darker and darker until it is like the back of
some sumptuous tapestry, an indecipherable palimps-
est which settles in the lower earth an invisible image
of glory. You might be out in a biting wind and
driving hail, checked by a covert from which no fox
will move, your toes and fingers numb with cold, and
the grey light fading into nothingness. But each kind
of weather has its own intimate story, and the worst
of weathers serves merely as a more emphatic frame
to horse and hound as they proceed with undimin-
ished joy about their business.

This indifference to the weather – or rather, joy in
the weather, in all its forms – was illustrated by my
first visit to the puppy show. Shows of hounds and
working terriers are among those mysteries of the
field, which are revealed only bit by bit and after long
initiation, but which contain some fragment of the
ineffable meaning of the chase. The hound puppies
from the hunt kennels have hitherto been scattered
around the neighbourhood in farms and cottages,
there to be 'walked' by country families charged with
the formation of their physique and character. It is
not only the hound who is judged, therefore, but the

walker who created him out of shapeless dog-stuff,
and who anxiously struts in the wings at the puppy
show like an Edwardian mother at her daughter's
coming out.

It is at the puppy show that breeding skills are put
to their first test. Foxhounds have the longest of all
recorded pedigrees, and the eighteenth- and nineteenth-century literature abounds in descriptions –
still pored over by the cognoscenti, for whom this is
the highest poetry – of the special qualities of once-
famous breeding hounds. Huntsmen and masters
come to the show from other packs, some to judge
and some to observe, with a view to enhancing the
gene pool over which they preside. For a moment we
enter into the mystery of nature's renewal. There is a
sense of subdued celebration, calling to mind those
ancient festivals of rebirth – of Isis and Osiris,
Astarte, Adonis and the Cyprian Venus. Not that the
English would go far in this direction. Only a
phlegmatic, sceptical sort of rejoicing is permitted:
muted grunts, a discreet but attentive scrutiny of
clothes and every now and then a quickly stifled bark
of fellow-feeling.

Animal shows are in fact an anachronism, in that
they encourage the thought that breeding matters,
that the virtues and vices of the father are passed to
the son, and that races may degenerate. Apply those
self-evident maxims to the human species, and you
will quickly find yourself an outcast. The umpteenth
Lord Willoughby de Broke, father of the gentleman
referred to at the beginning of this book, made the

point in the House of Lords in 1911: 'I have been brought up in the midst of stock-breeding of all kinds all my life,' he barked, 'and I am prepared to defend the hereditary principle ... whether the principle is applied to Peers or to foxhounds.' Not surprisingly, the hereditary principle did not gain any new subscribers from this particular defence of it.

The puppy show occurred on the one wet day in a summer of unnatural drought. Cascades of luke-warm water have poured all morning from a sultry sky, as though God were indolently splashing in his measureless bath upstairs. Rain is everywhere, briefly withholding only to pour more abundantly, in long splashing filaments which trail through the sky like the strings of mad balloons, tangling in umbrellas and dancing on the rims of bowler hats. The hats are raised in startled salutation, as the hunt followers, blinking at one another through the rain, recognize with a kind of bleary astonishment the faces which they normally see fierce and exultant in the field. The men wear summer suits with paisley-pattern ties, twirling their smart umbrellas above the heads of ladies in scant summer frocks, whose straw hats droop from the damp. The hunting farmers are there in heavy brown shoes and waterproofs, their wives wrapped tight in gaberdine.

A space has been roped off before the kennels, and here the people gather: peaceable farmers nodding sagely, hunt servants in bowler hats, eager widows with handbags clutched before them, leisured bankers in London suits, squires, soldiers, labourers and businessmen: all standing stiff, wet and contented in the pouring rain. Old Masters, new Masters and Masters-to-be form nuclei to which pastel-shaded girls attach themselves like petals, while ex-Master Lord Mancroft, splendid in his pale cream Al Capone mackintosh, flits from flower to flower, an endless flow of mellifluous hound-talk mingling with the rain that streams across his features.

Out of the swirling mist the judges appear: Michael Farrin, huntsman of the Quorn, and the legendary Captain Ronnie Wallace, peering from eyes which bulge like crystal orbs, and waving the rain aside as though it had no business to be there. 'Captain', I had already discovered, is the favoured rank for a Master of Fox Hounds: just exalted enough to confer authority in the field, but not so grand as to damage the web of equality which emerges from the common danger, and not so senior as to imply that military duties had so far taken precedence over hunting.

The kennel doors clang open and the first couple of hounds emerge: Freeman and Freestone are their names, walked, according to the programme, by Miss Archer. It is hard to decide which is the more English: the names of the hounds – Grappler and Grasper, Walnut and Wattle, Bracken and Bracket, Guilty and Gusty, Willow and Wishful – or those of their walkers – Miss Archer, Miss Calcot, Mrs Manners, Mrs Dibble, the Dickensian Miss Spawkes and the Surteesian Miss Gawthropp, who is responsible for Gulliver, the winning doghound.

The naming of hounds is an ancient science. For whatever cause, a dog will gradually adapt his behaviour to his name, and will understand, from the likeness of hound-names, that he has a dual nature, as individual and as part of the team. (Hence hounds are always counted in couples, to emphasize that a single hound is incomplete.) Beckford devotes several pages to a list of names; so does Nicholas Cox in the previous most popular hunting manual, composed a century earlier; so too does Xenophon in his treatise on hunting. And although none of this makes sense to an outsider, it should be seen as a distillation, in rude and rustic poetry, of the long triumphant history of our species-bond.*

Captain Wallace stands in the ring, his intent eyes following every flexion of the muscles with the same absorption as the hounds will follow their fox. The water pours unceasingly from the rim of his bowler hat, making a curtain of beads around his plum-coloured face, and a water-logged Barbour clings to his arm as he points to a hound to promote or downgrade him. People draw closer, allowing their umbrellas gradually to fall to one side. Rain entirely films their bodies, soaking their festive clothes, filling

---

* Ovid raises this poetry to ten-fold heights in *Metamorphoses*, Book 3, lines 206–27, where he lists the names of Actaeon's hounds as one by one they settle on the scent of their master. Hunting people will grasp the full poignancy of this passage, for they will read the list of names as an inventory, rehearsed in terror, of a simple but ineradicable love. Ted Hughes, *Tales from Ovid*, pp. 109–10, captures the spirit well.

mouths and eyes and ears and causing streams of make-up to run down stoical clown-like faces. The clouds thicken and a long dismal thunder rolls in the distance. We are ankle-deep in water, the hounds scarcely visible as they snatch up their water-logged biscuits. And still we murmur our comments, consult our smeared programmes, and nod our quiet approval as the judges' dripping arms extend.

The atmosphere is a curious mixture of intensity and nonchalance, and the veil of rain which covers everything acts like a soft-focus lens, casting the scene backwards into history. The carefully coloured figures, the rigid postures, the meticulous refusal to be excited, which communicates itself even to the hounds as they step into the ring with aloof English dignity – all this reminds me of an Edwardian postcard, faded now, with many details rubbed away and indecipherable, and yet unmistakable in its eccentric life. What, I wonder, would a foreigner make of this scene – so subdued and stoical in its pleasure, so quiet and mad and English?

If I could attend a puppy show in the pouring rain, during those summer weeks when I should be writing, this was a sign that I too was mad. But it didn't worry me. By now I had decided to move to the country, where I would share my life with George. Having recently won another libel action, to the tune of seventy-five grand, I took leave of my senses, and went in search of a cottage, a field and a new career.

'Only if we are capable of dwelling, only then can

we build.' So writes Heidegger, though he might as
well have said that only when we are capable of
building, only then can we dwell. Either way, his
thought contains the truth about modern architecture, which is an architecture of people who no
longer build for the sake of dwelling. The modern
city, with its through-roads and street-lights and
shopping centres, with its industrial parks and office
towers, is nothing but the waste thrown down by
careless nomads. Such is Swindon, that monstrous
dump of undwelling in the heart of England, brought
into being precisely by the desire to be somewhere
else. Not satisfied with trains, people turned to cars,
and Swindon followed suit. Now, on the outskirts of
the railway town, there stands a great Honda factory,
ceaselessly disgorging its products on to roads which
are already crammed so full of them that hardly
anything moves. A few hundred yards beyond the
factory lies Stanton Fitzwarren, a little village of
Cotswold stone, the possession of one family over
generations, eaten away at the extremities by the sale
of one house then another, damaged by the loss of its
resident vicar and the closing of its once-busy school,
but remaining until the sixties miraculously intact, its
great house still inhabited, the church beneath its
wing attended by the whole community, and the
string of stone cottages, which stretch down the
narrow road beyond the rectory, sheltering workers
from the house and farms. North Farm and South
Farm captured the surrounding land and tied it to
the village, with barns and out-buildings of mingled

brick and stone; while in front of the house stretched a park of old turf, where oaks and limes and wellingtonias rose to form a green background to the cottages, and across which there marched an avenue of elms, advancing to the seething edge of Swindon with the same heroic absurdity as that which sent the light brigade, led by the fox-hunting Lord Cardigan, into the Russian guns.

Those 'immemorial elms' have gone the way of Tennyson's England, destroyed by diseases from abroad; the council has filled in the gaps between the cottages with 'social' (which is to say, anti-social) housing, and the whole community has fallen apart as the result of events to which I owe my present happiness.

A dynasty, wrote Ibn Khaldun in the *Mutakallimah*, is a finite thing, rising to its height of power only to decline in self-doubt and indolence. Stanton Fitzwarren was inherited, at last, by a man incapable of living in or loving it, whose restless disaffection translated itself first into architectural projects that wiped away its kindly face, and then into a religious revulsion towards these helpless things of stone that still cried out for ownership. He gave the whole lot to the Unification Church, of which he had become a member, and went to live elsewhere.

Now I have nothing against the Unification Church, or its founder, the self-styled Reverend Moon, who strikes me as a normal oriental business-man, distinguished by the singular honesty with which he demands the life and soul of those who join

his firm. And I am additionally grateful to him for his
foresight in recruiting a hunting man to take charge
of the newly acquired estate. Jonathan had the dark
and untameable wildness of nature which comes with
a born love of horses, and had unfurled the leash of
his religion to its full extent, so as to live in Stanton
Fitzwarren as an English squire, breeding race-
horses, riding to hounds, entering for the point-to-
point, and striking deals with the canny instinct of a
man who gambles. Only the presence of a quiet
Japanese wife – bestowed on him by the Rev. Moon
as part of his policy of miscegenation – hinted at his
other and more mystical side. And when he suggested, as we galloped side by side over fences one
cold November day, that I might rent the cottage
which had been the schoolmaster's in the days when
Stanton's children still were taught, I leaped at the
chance.

George moved into the stables, and with him Jess
and Bob, acquisitions required by my obsession. Since
taking up hunting I have spent half my earnings on
horses and their upkeep, and not a penny have I
regretted – not even the £4,500 paid for Ginger,
who went lame on her first day out. I can now
understand those people who spend £10,000 on a
ticket for the world cup final, or as much again on a
magnum of Lafite.

There was something peculiarly exciting about life
in Stanton Fitzwarren – life on the very edge of the
ugliest town in England, in which people exist
without religion, history or culture, spending their

earnings on the Costa Brava, living for the windfall that never comes, and all the while, just a few fields away, the manners of old England upheld by dogged individualists, drawing the foxy outskirts of the town, and veering away with their prize to ancient pastures. Passing through this blazing hell I felt a surge of gratitude for my new life, that could so nearly mingle with the modern world and yet be free of it. I was a visitor from psychic space, consciously alien to this unconscious alienation, and settling down at last, in a feather-bed of inverted commas.

Outside the academy, I discovered, England is full of people like me. If Baudelaire's image of nature were never true before it is true today. The natural world has become a forest of symbols, and in this *selva oscura* the post-modern bodgers are at work, fashioning the living pillars of their imagination into pre-modern furniture. One such bodger is Bill Reid, owner and manager of the club in Swindon's steely heart, where young people dance away the night. Bill began life as a bass player, and there is something of the jauntiness of the jazz-band in his tranquil manner. He made his money in London, organizing pop concerts in a club, and securing, by a stroke of luck, the as yet undiscovered Rolling Stones. Now he has a farm, keeps cows and sheep and horses, has risen like John Jorrocks to be Master of Foxhounds, and bodged a rural life from urban fantasies. Nothing undermines his faith in human nature. He does not regard the youth who dance in his club as lost; somewhere, he believes, waiting to be discovered, is the unbroken thread of national sentiment which joins them to the quiet farmers with whom, as MFH, he must negotiate our passage.

Like everyone who presumes on human kindness, Bill is an optimist. And optimism, when moderate and scrupulous, is catching. In Monday country, over which he presides, the hunt is welcome. A Master must persuade the farmers to let us cross; he must mollify their rage at our mistakes, and make good the damage. All this requires hospitality: farmers' suppers and hunt breakfasts, Christmas parties, drinks in the pub and a bottle of whisky at the end of the day. No Master should presume on the good-will of his hosts or shirk the duty of reparation. Returning at the day's end to a farm where his field had disturbed a herd of cattle, Lord Mancroft was told 'you wash them off, since you made them dirty'. A wet cloth was thrown in his face; he picked it up, fetched a bucket, and worked until midnight, when the farmer gave a gruff 'goodnight'.

Bill's demotic manner spares him such humiliations. He exists at the point of intersection of 'little platoons', mixing with local people through the networks of rural society. Modern societies suffer from a deficit of membership. Adults used to help young people to join things: they ran scout troupes, youth clubs, cadets, drama groups, jazz bands, and orchestras; they introduced randy teenagers to reeling, writhing and fainting in coils. Now nobody bothers; the young are left to their self-made gangs and raves and discos, which offer no rite of passage to the adult world.

In country life, however, membership is the norm – much of it through the hunt. The pony club, the point-to-point, the fun rides and summer parties; the Hunt Ball and hunter trials, the farmers' suppers and supporters' club, the hunt breakfasts, barbecues, and lawn meets: into these events the joyous social energy of the hunt spills over, making a celebration and an institution out of neighbourliness. Bill is the epitome of this social energy, which he takes with him from the hunting field to the club in Swindon, like the optimist who took sealed barrels of light into a pitch-dark building, before the discovery of windows. And in this quiet, avuncular figure, the Swindon drop-outs find their truest counsellor.

It was Bill who first confirmed my outsider's vision of the huntsman. We had come to a check in a patch of scrub near the lovely village of Duntisbourne by Cirencester, and Sidney had taken the hounds to a hedgerow just beyond, making a circular cast. I remarked to Bill, who stood next to me, what a good huntsman Sidney is.

'One of the best in the country,' was his quick reply.

'There is something uncanny,' I went on, 'in his relation to the hounds – and to the fox as well.'

Bill responded with a confiding touch to the forearm, addressing me with kindly eyes through the upper lenses of his spectacles.

'Funny you should say that, but Sidney is only

happy when hunting, and happy in just the way a hound is happy. His father was a hunt servant, and so were both his grandfathers. His uncle was huntsman to the Quorn and he himself has spent his life in the kennels: he was even born there. When he is not hunting our hounds he is out with the Heythrop, and when our season is over he goes down to Exmoor to hunt stags through the summer. Not a day out of the saddle since he was a boy.

'And another thing. His wife told me that when the moon is full, he behaves in a most peculiar and mystical way, like a hound, and cannot easily be brought to his senses. She told me this in confidence and I am not to repeat it – but there you are, it bears out what you say entirely.'

By this time we were running after the fox that Sidney had winkled from its hiding place, and Bill was shouting at the top of his voice, so that all could hear. In hunt gossip, there is no such thing as confidentiality, and the unassuageable desire for information is fed from every source, however privileged.

In Grantley Berkeley's day farmers were not always so gracious as they are towards Bill Reid. Berkeley's hunt was followed by a cavalry of leisured toffs who, because they owned the land, could afford to trample on the crops of those who merely rented it. At the same time, the courts would protect the tenants, even when they attacked the horsemen with pitch-forks and spades, and award serious damages against the hunt and its master. Although a landed aristocrat and a Member of Parliament, Berkeley was, in his capacity as huntsman, at the mercy of people who lacked his social advantages and, to do him credit, he tried hard to mend his boyish ways.

Elsewhere the process of social emendation had broken down the wall of privilege. Already in 1830 'Nimrod' was devoting space in his snobbish column to the 'yeomen and graziers' of the field, mentioning among the followers of the Quorn a draper, a farrier and a list of characters known only by nicknames, such as 'Gameboy Hinton' and 'Wings'. Forty years later, in the 'Hunting Sketches' which he wrote for the *Pall Mall Gazette*, Trollope could truthfully describe the field as including 'attorneys, country bankers, doctors, apothecaries, maltsters, millers, butchers, bakers, innkeepers, auctioneers, graziers, builders, retired officers, judges home from India, barristers who take weekly holidays, stockbrokers, newspaper editors, artists and sailors.'

This process of social emendation is still visible in the hunt. English society grows like a fungus on the rotting margins, in the places where old meets new. The heart of rural life is not the country house, now surrendered to the tax-man and preserved in aspic by the National Trust. Nor is it the industrial farm, run on subsidies for the profit of anonymous bankers in the city. Nor is it the village, where retired stock-brokers endlessly wash their BMWs and upper-class hippies keep unprofitable goats. The heart of the country is the motorway. I don't mean the roaring metalled surface, where New Britons in their sealed

containers zoom above Old England's ruined fields. I
mean the humming arches beneath the road, the
scrubby horse-sick fields abutting it, the little plots
marked off with barbed wire, with their rotting sheds
and dismal shetlands. It is here that rural aspirations
start – where young girls come to feed their seedy
ponies, where shy old botanists breed useless plants,
where crashed cars are ransacked by would-be
mechanics and tinkers live in rusting mobile homes.
For in these places land is cheap, unwanted or
unowned, and the writ of planning only half-heart-
edly runs. It is here that you will find the cheap livery
yard in which to stable or purchase a horse. And
among the regulars there is sure to be a new Jack
Scruton, with a passion for wildflowers and Tyn-
dale's bible, who will stop you like the Ancient
Mariner and denounce the usurpation of his fore-
father's land.

Ibn Khaldun was right. If you want to know which
things are dying in the national culture, look at those
with wealth and leisure, whose brain-dead heirs
smoke dope in Georgian attics. If you want to know
what is most alive, look in those fertile muck-heaps
on the margins. People who associate hunting with
the landed gentry will naturally see it as a dying
habit. But hunting is more accurately associated with
the motorway arch, the pirate livery and that fiercest
and most territorial of motorway residents – the
seasonal groom.

She comes to you unannounced, and addresses you
without formality. She has heard that you have a

stable of hunters and offers her services for cash:
mucking out, tack-cleaning, exercise and transport,
all for less than the minimum wage. There is
something sharp, defensive and yet covertly vulner-
able in her manner, like a woman who has been often
wounded and won't stand for it again. Her hands are
clenched at her sides, and she stares at you with a
wide-eyed canny insolence: the message is that she
knows about men and is a match for them. She wears
trainers and jeans and a grubby nylon jacket, and it is
in this unequestrian costume that she leaps astride
your horse to show her skills.

At once her manner changes. A wistful, tender
expression crosses her features, and her body relaxes
into the saddle. Her fingers hold the reins like the
fingers of a mother round the wrist of a child. The
horse is alert, his ears forward, an expression of
pleased expectancy in his eyes. After a few circles in
the field, she comes back to the gate and says 'he's
lovely', as though it were the horse and not the rider
on trial. She goes through the stables, denouncing
each item of tack, each rug, each peg or hook or
saddle-rack. The place will have to be cleaned up, re-
arranged, and given a proper routine. And it's not fair
on a horse, she exclaims, to keep him on so little
straw, with this dusty hay and only two buckets of
water. Gradually she establishes her indispensability,
and you begin to thank your good fortune that she
turned up in the nick of time.

Three months later, in the middle of the season,
when grooms are no longer available, she will have

moved Arthur from the shed by the motorway and
installed him next to George, since it is part of the
deal, she claims, that she should have free livery for
her horse. On hunting days she will come early, give
a cursory grooming to George, and devote an hour
or more to polishing Arthur. She will then load them
both in the box, since it is also part of the deal that
her hunting costs should be paid by her employer. On
other days she turns up with a child – her guarantee
of council housing and welfare benefits, whose father
she hardly knew – it being part of the deal that the
poor little mite, who has no-one to look after him at
home, which is not much of a home in any case,
should be with his mum in a place where he can run
around and get some air. The child screams through
the yard, scaring animals, scattering the muck-heap,
and puking on the lawn, while in the over-heated
tack-room, to a background of grunge and techno-
rock, the groom entertains the shifting products of
the lottery culture: single mothers, idle boyfriends,
bungling handymen, who come to pass the time of
day between the social security and the pub.

Your tack is stiff and mud-encrusted; your horses
are suffering from strained ligaments, corns and
mud-fever; your stables are in disarray, with the rugs
half shredded, and the tools mislaid or broken. But
your reproaches are greeted with disdain: how could
you look after my lovely boys, and would it be fair on
them? Pay me as little as you like, only let me come
and see to them – I couldn't be happy if I thought
they were neglected.

Of course, not every groom is a New Briton. And in women, even post-modern women, horses awaken a vestigial sense of responsibility. Their simple needs, placid temperaments and warm, fragrant bodies; their incontinence, so innocent and unashamed like the incontinence of a baby; their very strength, which yields at once to the feminine touch – all these appeal to womanly instincts. By contrast, men are unreliable, untameable, with complicated needs and unsavoury smells. They fend too easily for themselves, and violate the natural order which places women higher than men in the scheme of things. In any contest between man and horse – and it is as such a contest that the girl groom views her job – the horse will win.

A great number of those who come hunting, perhaps even the majority, are women. And this is the real reason why hunting is so full of terrors, and why you need nerves of steel to cope with it. Most hunting women are dignified ladies, bound to each other and the world by a web of charitable concern. But in every hunt there are three or four women who act as self-appointed vigilantes, who devote themselves to scaring away newcomers, and who ensure that nobody feels at ease until properly humbled and maybe not even then.

Now it is undeniable that horses, in an excited herd, are dangerous. In their natural state – and hunting is a partial return to the natural state – they are fiercely competitive and protective of their space. Without the impediment of a rider, a horse will quickly yield space to the one who insists on it, or demand it from the one who stands in his way. But a bad rider will not respond as he should to these delicate equine signals. The result will be a vicious kick, made worse by the iron shoe.

We should also remember the evolutionary significance of obstacles. A lion pursuing the herd serves his own interest by killing the straggler, so minimizing risk. He also serves the interest of the herd, by taking the one who is least likely to enhance its genetic endowment. Apply a modicum of ethology to those facts, and you will understand why a horse, once it has made up its mind to jump, will try to do so at the first opportunity, and at the head of the queue. Unless carefully controlled, therefore, a horse will gallop in front of the one who is jumping.

Those and similar facts mean that everyone who hunts is a risk to his neighbours. The hunting harpie is the one who has made it her business to remind you of this. If your horse kicks out – however tentatively and from however far away – she will shout at you to take him away and beat the living daylights out of him. If you barge into her or ride across, she will pursue you with blood-curdling curses, designed to drive you in shame from the field. If your horse stops at a jump, she will shout 'For God's sake!' as though you were a mischievous child on a bowling green.

If, on the other hand, her horse kicks out at yours – and this is highly likely, since horses, like dogs, acquire the nature of their keepers – she will instantly turn round to berate you for getting too close. If she rides you off at a jump it will be with the cry of 'Get out of the way!' She will cut across you as she passes, shouting 'Do *please* mind my heels!' And if she particularly dislikes you, which is highly probable if you are a freak or a townie or a professor, she will make a point of being there at every jump, in order to press in ahead of you, or swear at you for doing the same.

Some people explain the hunting harpie with reference to nerves. Women, they say, feel more fear in these stressful occasions, and respond with what are really cries of alarm, mistaken by the chivalrous ear for curses. I don't agree with this. Women are fearless riders; and it is not alarm but aggression that you hear when they turn on you. I would therefore offer a more Darwinian explanation. It is in the nature of men in danger to co-operate, by forming an unspoken web of comradeship. Hence when one man rides off another, both tend to apologize. This apologetic instinct is fundamental to the hunter-gatherer, and it is the instinct that makes armies possible. Danger enhances the masculine capacity to live with faults, since it is only thus that danger can be vanquished. In a crisis women will tolerate nothing less than total competence from the men at their side, and the small adjustments are never made. And here is the true reason why women ought not to fight in armies – that, in the moment of supreme danger, they might turn their hostility as much on their comrades as their foes.

The hunting harpie provides a barrier to membership, an ordeal which the novice must survive. A
harpieless hunt would lack the self-policing character
that ensures survival. Whatever the humiliation,
therefore, the newcomer must learn to stutter out his
apologies and go away smarting with shame. Nothing less than this is required.

I do not judge all hunting women by the harpie,
any more than I judge all politicians by Dennis
Skinner or Tony Banks, equally necessary though
such hooligans are, to the proper functioning of the
House of Commons. The hunting field exemplifies an
all-but-forgotten ideal – the 'unity in variety' which
inspired the art of Hogarth and the landscape
gardening of Capability Brown. Side by side with the
groom from the motorway rides the not-quite-
famous actress, the farming spinster, the lady barris-
ter and next year's answer to the Spice Girls. And
above them all, bobbing side-saddle over hedges on a
massive horse, there flies an 85-year-old lady who
lives alone in her vast ancestral home. She resembles
a tiny porcelain doll, precariously balanced on this
heaving animal, seemingly strengthless, inflexible
and at any moment about to tumble to the ground;
maintaining nevertheless a self-imposed regime of
rank and caste and courtesy, refusing to accept the
form or appearance that nature has bestowed, casting
herself anew as Idea or symbol, and – for all that –
miraculously in control of the earthbound monster on
which she sways and which will one day, without
warning, send her tumbling to the ground. She is the

living symbol of Reason and its fate, and if you wish to understand our species, its hope and transcendence and tragedy, then you should observe this cool untroubled figure, as it bounces high in the air from the side of the jumping horse, to be miraculously re-united with it as though attached by the finest of threads. Here is the proof that elegance, appearance and grace defy corruption, and that death, when it comes, is part of the comedy. And that is why women are so important a part of hunting: the *ewig weibliche* appears here in its lowest and its highest guise.

Shortly after settling in Stanton Fitzwarren, I began my new life, taking unpaid leave from the university, and devoting myself to writing. I began work on a philosophical novel in dialogue form, which was later published as *Xanthippic Dialogues*. One of the characters – Phryne, the scandalous courtesan of ancient Athens – greatly intrigued me, and I read widely in the sources to find the life and the style that were hers. I became fascinated by the Oxyrynchus papyri, and the glimpses that they offer of high art and recipes, philosophy and fornication, religion and make-up all mingled by the shifting desert sands. I was puzzling over Phryne by a covert near Hannington, where the hounds had come to a check. I wanted her to interrupt a symposium with the cry of 'knickers!' But ancient Greek has no word for this modern garment.

The young woman next to me, a visitor from some neighbouring hunt, insisted on talking: something about her horse, which was no longer young.

Normally, when a woman begins to talk about her
horse, I slink away out of earshot. But it makes a
difference when the speaker quotes from Sophocles:

> Like the well-bred horse who, though old,
> In time of battle does not lose his spirit
> But pricks up his ears.*

Her horse was doing just that, since the hounds had
begun to speak. She was a Greek scholar, engaged in
post-doctoral research. My interest quickened. I
asked her what she studied. And yes, she even looked
like Phryne – saucy eyes, sensual lips, a laughing
haughty countenance.

'I'm a papyrologist,' she proudly answered.

A papyrologist! A thousand urgent questions
crowded into my mind. The papyrus about child-
exposure, when would she date it? The one about
Lastheneia of Mantinea: is it genuine? The fragments
of the satyr play, have they been added to? But
Sidney was shouting 'Tally-ho', the hounds were
shooting through the brown sedge like silver bullets,
the stampede was on. Her old horse went flying to
the front of the field.

'What is the Greek for "knickers"?' I shouted after
her.

'That I *don't* know,' she shouted back, but without
turning to me, since her horse was galloping towards
a hedge.

* *Electra*, 25–7.

We ran for half an hour, and when I sought for her she had vanished. Nor did she ever reappear with the VWH. Nevertheless, she implanted in my mind the novel idea that there might be, somewhere in this frothy horse-borne sea of female faces, the future Mrs Scruton.

Finding her took several years. Meanwhile I addressed the task in hand, which was hunting. I kept a diary of my early exploits, and I include two extracts here, the first because it illustrates the phlegmatic temper of the VWH, the second because it records my first encounter with the region near Malmesbury where I was eventually to settle down. Both were written before I moved to Stanton Fitzwarren, when I was teaching in the evenings at Birkbeck College.

4th November 1989, Saturday. Second horses. Mounting George I fall off, as he impatiently peels away after the field. Second time lucky, but almost at once a vicious hail-storm begins. I can see nothing, while George, furiously plunging on, crashes constantly into the animal in front. I am tired, he is strong, eager and bewildered, and I am greatly impressed by his immense size and the distance that I may soon have to fall.

Suddenly the storm passes, the sun nose-dives through the last flapping curtain of rain, and the clouds break apart and reassemble, magnificent towers of opalescent blue and grey. We return by degrees to the team-chase course, where George –

who is stiff in the back leg from a barbed-wire
injury – jumps high and sudden over successive
fences, including a post and rail on to the road
followed by a high brush off it where I nearly lose
balance. Then we queue for what seems to be a
tiny jump at the bottom of the wood, in a boggy
track leading to open country. Yet a wooden rail is
concealed in the brush at the top of it and first one
horse, then another, catches his hind legs. One
comes down, throwing the little girl who is riding
it. She lies still for some time until adult comfort
arrives. Fighting back tears, she gets to her feet
and hobbles off, to be reunited with her animal.
Then Satman tumbles, runs around winded with
an agonized look as we retrieve his pony, and has
just reassumed his serene Indian expression when
a third horse catches the rail, rises up in the air,
turns languorously over, and comes down on its
back, the rider beneath it, clutching at the air with
helpless hands.

The horse squirms like a great sack of entrails
on the buried form of the man, who releases
desperate muffled cries, becoming quieter and
quieter as the horse grinds him into the earth. The
animal finally rights itself, staggers to its feet, and
trots off after the other horses. An awful silence
ensues as we contemplate the crumpled figure in
the grass. Cyril, the senior outrider who used to be
Lord Bathurst's groom, and who must have seen a
thing or two in his time, rides up beside me and
says, '*He's* dead I reckon.' Whereupon he takes a

pipe from his pocket and begins serenely packing it with tobacco, sagely nodding at the awful scene. But the figure begins to move, rises to its knees, falls forward, rises again, and is now being helped to its feet. 'Sorry. Alright in a moment. Just a bit winded.' So saying he collapses entirely and is carried away unconscious from the field. I relax my hold on the rein and George, who has been snorting and stamping with impatience, seizes his chance and gallops after the hounds.

20th December 1989, Wednesday. Meet at Little Somerford near Malmesbury. The country in this part is very different: hedges and pastures to the north of the Swindon-Malmesbury Road, arable land in the valley to the south of it. Uninterrupted rain over several days has flooded the fields, in which isolated farms and manors stand amid clumps of trees.

George is sluggish as we move off into the valley. The river Avon flows through here, scarcely more than five yards wide. Little scent, but the frequent jumps excite the horses, so that we move around the country as though in hot pursuit of nothing. As the morning ends we enter a beautiful section of the valley, where a Victorian railway viaduct in violet brick marches across the pasture and takes a double stride above the Avon. We squeeze along a narrow slippery track beneath the arches and cross more pasture, where there are agitated cows, into gorse and scrub on a rise below Maunditts Park Farm. The sun is still shining, although in the distance, passing over to the east of us, squalls of zinc-coloured rain-cloud trail strings of mist across the grey-green countryside. Before us on the next hill top, shining like the Holy City, is Malmesbury, an unspoilt cluster of lime-stone houses, with a nail-like spire, bluish rooftops and the abbey lying in ruins at its apex like the ark of Noah on Mount Sinai. Yellow sunlight pours over the countryside around the town, and the blue-grey clouds in the distance seem to be made of the same substance as the houses: the soft, plastic matter of creation, uncorrupted, pliable, folding and forming in obedience to the will of God. Below us the Avon meanders through the valley, its banks obscured by copses, finding its way to Malmesbury and onwards to the sea. England appears to us now and then – but in a kind of dream, a floating fragment of the greatness that has gone.

A fox jumps from the barn at Maunditts Park Farm, and stupidly runs downhill into the wind. We encourage it in the opposite direction, but it insists on the gorse, where it is instantly cornered and killed. This pleases the hounds, and therefore the huntsman; but it does not please the field. We cross over into the hedge-strewn country around Lea Wood, and the rain arrives. George is now going very strong, dancing into each field of grass and sailing smoothly over the tiger-traps. But the relentless rain pours down, and we find nothing until three o'clock, in the beautiful stone grotto which is Chink Farm – a name and a place out of Tolkien, where gnomes clutch wooden bowls of mare's milk, seated around a millstone table.

We circle this place several times; over one jump, which George miscalculates, I fall off as he swivels in the air. And then, when we are soaked through, and visibility has terminally declined, the Master (Mrs Barker) calls it a day, since conditions now are dangerous. Unfortunately, to regain the road, we must jump over four successive tiger-traps into fast fields of pasture, and the horses are in no mood to go slowly. Water is flowing over everything, making a lubricating film over saddle, stirrup leathers, stirrups and George; riding him is like sitting astride a rapidly melting jelly. Over the first jump my stirrups slide straight out of their brackets and I land without them, staying on, not knowing what has happened, as George, refusing to stop, shakes me almost to death in the saddle. I recover from this, but at the next jump one of the stirrup leathers slips out of its clasp and begins to unwind. It is now too late to stop George, who is pointed at the third jump and going forward like the wind. I fall off on the far side, and watch him go on, galloping past the horse in front and taking the lead, riderless, over the final tiger-trap into the road. We find him later by the hunt box, looking very pleased with himself.

The Dibbles kindly take me home and lend me clothes belonging to 'Uncle George' – a dapper

sporting sort of farmer, judging by his outfit, who
died twenty years ago. After hot strong tea and
banana bread, I make for Swindon station and the
train to London. I give a lecture on Kant's theory
of time as the 'form of inner sense', wearing a
baggy sports jacket with padded shoulders and
maroon-coloured checks, trousers with belligerent
turn-ups which reach only half way down my
shins, and great brown shoes with lacquered toe-
caps. Someone has written 'Time is the form of
innocence' on the blackboard.

I passed through Malmesbury two years later,
having been invited for the first time to hunt with the
Beaufort. In the back of the lorry that I drove was
Ginger the mare, recovered now and pawing the
rubber matting with excitement. My nerves were
none too good. Compared with the Beaufort, I had
been told, the VWH is as lively as a show of prize
marrows.* Still, there were enough little cottages
for sale, and, as I drove anxiously by them, I
conceived the ambition to acquire one before I spent
all my money on horses and dissidents – both of
them, I discovered, black holes in one's pocket.

The meet was near Sherston, on the edge of the
Badminton estate, and surrounded by hunt-preserved

* For the record's sake, let me say that the judgement is
entirely false, and that, in the right country and with the right
scenting conditions, the VWH compares with any pack that I
have known.

pastures. (So famous is Sherston among fox-hunters, that Siegfried Sassoon chose this name for the hero of his *Memoirs of a Fox-hunting Man.*) Two hundred mounted followers had assembled, and since the eagerness of a horse rises exponentially with the size of the herd, Ginger was uncontrollable. Within minutes the huntsman, Captain Farquhar, had found a fox, and was greeting it with a rhythmical horn-call that sent Ginger into spasms of delirious excitement.

The chase was on. Bodies were strewn over the pastures, riderless horses neighed on the horizon, and soon the siren of an ambulance was ghosting the horn in eerie counterpoint. To my amazement I was still aloft, Ginger pushing to the front but not yet getting there, jumping rails and walls and hedges, and at one point coming face to face with an obstacle which must surely be the end of us both: a horse which had come to its knees before the very wall at which Ginger had set her unstoppable muzzle. She jumped both horse and wall and flew on, to loud and justified protests. This, the most frightening day of my life since those two secret policemen had stepped from behind a bush in Brno, was soon brought to an end, with the return of Ginger's lameness.

Some time afterwards I found the little farmhouse near Malmesbury, on the edge of the Beaufort country, from where I can hunt with both packs of hounds. Thanks to Barney, trained as a master's horse, I was beginning to get the measure of those Beaufort Saturdays. Unfortunately, Barney, who never lost his head, sometimes lost his legs, which

were becoming stiff and wooden behind. But this too
was a blessing. For it was thanks to these legs that
the future Mrs Scruton was discovered.

As part of my attempt to break with the academic
world, I had accepted an offer from Boston University, to teach there every autumn for a salary which
would keep me alive for the year. To miss the season
was unbearable. Each Friday, therefore, I would
board the plane in Boston, and, urged on by
prevailing winds, arrive in Heathrow in time for the
meet at Badminton. Madness? Not at all. Jet-lag is
dispelled by hunting, winter fares are cheap, and,
because nothing ever happens in America, you spend
no money there, save on the attempt to make things
happen. Moreover, the attempt is futile; hence those
who try to amuse themselves in America spend far
more than I ever did on fleeing to the hunting field in
England.

On one of these mornings I was introduced to a
quiet girl whose delicate features deeply appealed to
me, and whose eyes seemed full of a quizzical interest,
as though surprised by light. She had just graduated
from university and, when I explained my profession,
she told me about her own academic interests, and
asked whether she should study for a doctorate. I was
thinking in a worried way about my student Seth,
with his gentle stutter, avoiding eyes and octaves of
silver ear-rings, who devoted all his days and nights
to a thesis on Samuel Beckett. His purpose in this was
to take revenge on his father, a big cheese in the State
Department. But Seth took no revenge and little joy

in his unfinishable studies. Like Beckett's tetchy characters, he would peel away the onion of his life, until only a mute subjective nothingness remained.

Not if you can avoid it, was my advice to Sophie. She took my advice, and went to work for a publisher in London.

A few weeks later, out hunting with the Beaufort, Barney lost his legs on a slippery corner and came crashing down. I retrieved the horse, and the hunt went on. But one person stayed behind to help me, losing precious minutes which might ruin her day, and that was Sophie. Alert, considerate and poised, she overcame with a few deft words my fear of hunting women. The crazy thought entered my head, that in these bright young eyes there shone a soul as pre-modern as mine.

Thereafter we would meet each week in London, taking turns to cook dinner, offering support and encouragement – I to a life that was starting, she to a life that was starting again. Three months later, at the end of the season, Barney's legs again betrayed him. He hit a rail with his front feet, and somersaulted over me. As I fell through the air beneath him, in that infinite thin slice of time, I made my most important decision. If I live through this, I will ask her to marry me. Two days later Sophie visited me at home, where I lay with broken ribs, and I saw from her eyes that there was no need to ask.

That summer I resigned from Boston, and we set out on our life together.

CHAPTER FIVE

End?

Thanks to hunting, my life began again. But is hunting finished? Many think so; many hope so; many fear so. Hunting is not only an institution; it is a controversy, and an ancient one, already familiar to Plato, whose defence of the sport, in *The Laws*, is a model of applied philosophy.

No sooner had fox-hunting established itself as the 'Englishman's peculiar privilege' than it was dismissed as the anachronistic pastime of a dying caste: so quickly are traditions invented and destroyed. In their attacks on the Corn Laws, Cobden and Bright saw themselves as confronting the entire rural economy – a subsidized economy, then as now. To the new captains of industry the land-owners represented feudal arrangements which stood in the way of progress and free trade; Cobden castigated fox-hunting as the sign and symbol of rural backwardness. It was left to the only revolutionary among the Manchester mill-owners to seize the opportunity presented by industrial success. While lamenting the condition of the English working class, Friedrich Engels spent the vast profits which came from exploiting them on vintage claret, and took up hunting as his life's reward.

During the course of the last century, however, the argument shifted. Fox-hunting came to exemplify an old and shameful relation to the animal kingdom, a relation which, with the advent of Darwinism and the loss of religious faith, could no longer be decently sustained. Increasingly those who opposed the sport began to see it not as anachronistic but as cruel, even criminal. As I write, a Private Member's Bill lies before Parliament proposing (not for the first time in recent decades) to make fox-hunting into a crime. It is very unlikely to become law; but many people, perhaps the majority, will regret this. What justification can be offered, in these enlightened days, for a sport which so crucially depends upon the fear and flight of an animal, and which so often ends in that animal's death? The Private Member who has proposed the bill is a competition angler. But, for reasons which owe nothing to consistency and everything to sentiment, the prolonged pain and terror of the fish caught on a line awaken little or no sympathy in the hearts of those who grieve for the hunted fox, and are regarded as the unavoidable and legitimate cost of a beautiful pastime. And so they are.

Shortly after Michael Foster, Labour MP for Worcester, announced the intention to present his Bill, a rally occurred in Hyde Park, attended by over 100,000 people. It was the largest rally recorded in that place, and remarkable for the peaceable and genial

nature of those who came to it. Some had walked
from Wales, Scotland and Cornwall, in a show of
determination that took the public by surprise; many
were in London for the first time; most had never
been to a demonstration before, being the very
opposite of the slogan-chanting brow-beating type
that would naturally resort to displays of collective
protest by way of imposing their opinions on the rest
of us. These were ordinary country people, awoken
from their routines by Mr Foster, and determined to
show that hunting could not be abolished without
seriously damaging their lives.

But it says something about this new country of
ours that Parliament remained largely unmoved by
the spectacle. The House of Commons was packed for
the Bill's second reading, while only eleven members
turned up in the afternoon to consider educational
provision for the disabled. Hunting is high on the
activist agenda: higher than global warming, higher
than crime, higher than Rwanda or Saddam Hussein.
For this is how the suicide of nations begins, when
sentimentality prevails over sense.

Du calme, mon vieux! I admit that the English
sentimentality over animals is rather endearing. But
it is also a vice. Animals cannot answer back. They
cannot puncture our illusions. They allow us complete freedom to invent their feelings for them, to
project into their innocent eyes a fantasy world in
which we are the heroes, and to lay our phoney
passions before them without fear of a moral rebuke.

They are the easy option for the emotionally deprived.

In any case, moral questions are settled by thought, not emotion. Hitler stirred the passions of the German people, invoking nature, tradition and the land. A wonderful nostalgic vision gripped his followers, one of whom was Heidegger. The philosopher imagined that the great homecoming was at hand: the soil with all its dead would be restored to the people, and an old, honourable, earth-bound life would repossess the stolen soul of Germany. The Führer had other ideas. Having secured his pre-modern following, he moved on to modern warfare. His *Wandervogel* sentimentality led to a ban on hunting – the first in the civilized world – but also to the de-civilizing of Germany.

Tocqueville and Mill warn us against the 'tyranny of the majority' that would settle each question by a vote. Modern Britain is far from the mass hysteria of Nazi Germany. But the two countries resemble each other in this – that majority sentiment is used to justify measures which destroy minorities, by taking away the things for which they live. That is how we should see a ban on fox-hunting, and why we should take the controversy seriously, even if we don't much care about foxes or the people who hunt them.

Here, very briefly, is how I see the question. Animals are not moral beings: they have neither rights nor duties, they are not sovereign over their lives, and they can commit no crimes. If they *were* moral beings, then Kant's categorical imperative would apply to them: it would be wrong to kill them, capture them, confine them, harm them, or curtail their freedom. But it would also be wrong for *them* to do these things. Lions would be murderers, cuckoos usurpers, mice burglars, and magpies thieves. The fox would be the worst of living criminals, fully deserving the death penalty which we from time to time administer. For foxes kill not only for food, but with a wanton appetite for death and destruction. In short, to treat animals as moral beings is to mistreat them – it is to make demands which they could not satisfy, since they cannot understand them as demands.

It does not follow, however, that we can treat animals as we wish. For morality has many sources. We are commanded to do our duty; but we must also exercise compassion. And we should behave towards the natural world with piety, for we are its present trustees. Animals confuse us – especially wild animals – because they lie at the place where piety and pity compete. Pity elevates the individual over the species; piety requires us to save the species, even at the individual's cost. Nowhere is this conflict more vivid than in hunting. When a beaten fox, driven from covert into the open, sees that he cannot cross to safety and so turns back to his death, his despairing movements are unutterably pitiable. His eyes are no longer alert, his crafty expression has vanished, and in his down-turned panting mask you see 'alle þe wo on lyue' – and no expression that I have ever observed on an animal's face so perfectly matches those words. In that moment the individual is all: for unlike the species he must die. If you could save him, you would. And you know that it is not what is worst, but what is best in people, that makes them leap to the fox's defence in this predicament.

Even Sir William Bromley Davenport, Victorian author of 'The Old Meltonian' and other stirring ballads, was susceptible to this feeling. 'I confess,' he wrote, 'when alone I have come across the hiding place of a "beaten" fox, and he has, so to speak, confided his secret to me with big upturned and indescribably appealing eye, it has been sacred to me; I have retired softly, and rejoiced with huge joy when the huntsman at last calls away his baffled pack.'

If you are rational, however, you do not give the last word to pity. The hunt has run its course, and this fox will die. His death will be quick — quicker by far than the death of a mouse in the paws of a cat, of a rat in the jaws of a terrier or of a human in the hands of his doctor. He was given his chance, and he used his natural powers in a natural environment against a natural foe. If foxes are to be hunted, then some will be caught. The kill is the goal of hunting, and the single-minded motive of the hounds; to call them off at the moment of triumph, when all their intelligence, energy and skills have been deployed for this very moment, is to betray the relation on which hunting depends — the relation of trust between huntsman and hounds. You can do it once or twice — and all huntsmen will call their hounds away from a preg-nant vixen; to pursue such a creature, Beckford rightly says, 'is unnatural and cruel'. But if you call hounds away repeatedly, they will lose all heart for the chase, and that will be the end of your hunting.

The first question, therefore, is whether foxes would be better off in a world where they were not hunted. Would they, in such a world, enjoy a happier life, an easier death, and a greater toleration from those whose interests they threaten? I raised this question with Jim Barrington, then President of the League against Cruel Sports, after meeting him at a debate. Neither of us could answer it with confidence. In the course of subsequent discussions, however, when we became friends, we found ourselves agreeing that the fox will gain nothing from the abolition of hunting. Jim had the honesty to say this in public. He was thrown out of his job and horribly vilified by people whose morality seems not to extend beyond a concern for the lower animals.

The question I put to Jim is a technical one. I could not, in the space of this chapter, persuade you that the fox *is* better off where he is hunted. But you should bear in mind that hunting, as I have described it, is two different things – a task entrusted to a huntsman, and a sport engaged in by the rest. The sportsman, unlike the person charged with pest-control, hopes for abundant and healthy quarry, and has an ethic of fair play. One of the many myths propagated about fox-hunting is that the chase is deliberately prolonged, so as to generate the maximim pleasure for the riders. In fact, the fox is given the chance to save himself, before the pack is put on his traces. Thereafter the hounds are in the business of shortening, not lengthening, the chase. And if the fox goes to ground (unless in some made-made drain or dug-out), he must be left there; or, if the farmer objects to his presence, he should be dug out and shot.

If you consider all the many human interests that come together in that sequence of events, you will surely conclude that hunting with hounds might offer the fox the best form of coexistence with humans, who have no other motive to protect him or to conserve his habitat. And there is a deeper point. Shooting discriminates against bold, out-going, energetic and healthy animals, who are the most likely to be afoot in the open. Hunting discriminates against the old and diseased. For it is not easy to catch a healthy fox; it requires the concerted skill and power of three distinct species, and even so the chances lean heavily in the fox's favour.

It is often said that there is a contradiction in this defence of hunting. For how can hunting be justified as a means of controlling foxes, when it is also justified as a means of conserving them? But the contradiction is only apparent. Although fox-hunts do not account for many deaths (less than shooting or snaring, less by far than the traffic on country roads), they provide a motive for conservation, together with a selective cull. Hunting disperses foxes from the places where they do most damage, while allowing the real nuisances to be pin-pointed and killed. In the last century Masters would

compensate farmers for the loss of poultry and lambs,
rather than give them a motive to go out with a shot-
gun. Now they offer a reduced subscription to the
hunt.

And here is another reason why fox-hunting
should not be condemned, just because it is a sport.
Traditional forms of hunting have an ethic of combat.
The sportsman has a special respect for his quarry
and a desire to offer a fair chance in the contest
between them. Not that the animals appreciate this
chivalrous behaviour, which they themselves could
never emulate. But it is a part of human virtue − a
shadow version of the justice that we owe to our kind
− and only a vicious hunter would use every means in
his power to gain his prize. We see this clearly in
angling; we see it in shooting and hunting. And we
see it in football, boxing and cricket. It is through
contest that morality is learned; and that is why,
when the curriculum was invented by the Greeks,
sport was at the heart of it.

However, to call hunting a sport is to give a
hostage to fortune. It is to awaken both the instinctive hostility of the English puritan towards pleasure
and the illusion that in this case the pleasure is
sadistic. Roy Hattersley put the point well, in a
newspaper article:

> . . . the real objection to fox-hunting is the pleasure
> that the hunters get out of it . . . If killing foxes is
> necessary for the safety and survival of other
> species, I − and several million others − will vote

for it to continue. But the slaughter ought not to be fun.

It seems to me nevertheless that the objection is misplaced. The suffering of the caught fish is not fun, but the unwanted price of fun. To describe it as fun is to imply that the angler takes pleasure *in* the suffering, whereas in fact he takes pleasure *in spite of* the suffering. If there were a sport, exactly like angling except that the fish were lifted from the water and then tortured with hooks to the amused shrieks of the bystanders, we should regard it in quite another moral light from the sport of angling, however little it might differ in the perception of the fish. Likewise, if there were a sport which consisted in capturing and then torturing a fox, where the goal were precisely to inflict this suffering, we should all agree with Roy Hattersley's judgement. However, the pleasure of hunting comes in spite of death, and not because of it.

Some people, Jim Barrington included, believe that the use of terriers breaches this principle, being often a source of gleeful and sadistic delight to those engaged in it. This view looks credible, if we study the old literature on hunting. Here is Nicholas Cox, writing in 1674, explaining how to train a terrier to fight, by putting the dog in a cage with a cruelly mutilated fox:

Cut away the nether jaw, but meddle not with the

other, leaving the upper to show the fury of the
Beast, although it can do no harm therewith...

And it is true that there remains a kind of low-life
relation between man and dog which would find
nothing objectionable in Cox's nonchalant counsel.
But the flak-jacketed readers of *Snarl* and *Evil Dog*
engage in savage pursuits which have long been
illegal in this country. And no true terrier-man is
among them. The terrier-man is bound by the rules
of hunting, must discourage those underground
fights which lesser mortals overhear with relish, and
is there to ensure that the genuine pests, when they
have gone to ground, can be driven out and shot
humanely.

Being a member of a persecuted minority, I am
sensible of the need to be tolerant of sports which for
me have no personal appeal. But I cannot help
thinking that shooting and angling, for all their
beauty, have a moral downside. For is there not
something unsporting in the use of guns and hooks
against creatures with no natural understanding of
such things, and no defences against them? Shooting
and angling seem to me too much like *hubris*,
swaggering displays of a prowess made possible by
mere machinery. And when I read of those trips of
American 'hunters' into the wilderness, there to fire,
from the safety of a four-by-four, at some terrified cat
in a tree, and to gloat in triumph as the victim drops
to the ground in agony, I am thankful that the word
'hunting', properly used, denotes no such barbarous

practice, but only the noble recreation that I have described in this book — the hunting and following of hounds. This sport has none of the Buffalo-Billish bluster that has discredited the hunting of big game. No gun or trap or hook gives easy advantage to the hunter. For the hunter is a dog, who works as a member of a pack. Nothing that the fox encounters lies outside his natural repertoire of defences, and it is only by the greatest concentration of effort that the pack will be able at the last to pull him down.

I would not for a moment question the motives of those who are opposed to hunting. Nevertheless, it puzzles me that they should have singled out an activity in which animals and humans, working in happy companionship, are fully and magnificently alive, and in which no suffering occurs that is not part of nature's due. Do the protestors trouble themselves, I wonder, over the factory farms, where pigs and chickens are grown like vegetables for the sake of their meat? One glance into these fermenting seas of misery would cure people of the illusion that they live on morally respectable terms with the rest of nature. As in Nazi Germany, however, eyes are averted, lest the conscience be stirred. The camps are windowless and silent, hidden behind trees and known only by their smell. No protestors surround them, or vilify those who own and work in them. Many who shout and scream at the hunt happily eat the tortured limbs of battery chickens. Pigs which have never seen the light of day, which have never run or rootled or rubbed their backs on trees, which have never turned round, but merely stared in mad perplexity at the metal bars which trap them, are served in the restaurant of the House of Commons. And not one of those members who parade their tender conscience over fox-hunting has protested at the crime.

In all this controversy, however, there is another and in my view far more urgent question, which is that of country life itself. At the heart of everyone's idea of England is the image of our countryside, idealized, idyllized, idolized, even ordealized, but always emphatically there. Were it not for this idea, English art and music would hardly exist. Were it not for country life, our literature – from George Eliot to Enid Blighter, as Jack Scruton called her, from *A Midsummer Night's Dream* to *The Archers* – would lack its distinctive subject-matter. But the English countryside is not a slice of untilled nature. It is a human institution, built over centuries, in the image of the people who made it. It has been damaged in many ways: by the flight to the industrial towns, by the vandalism of agribusiness, by the death through taxation of the landed estates, by the post-war assault on hedgerows and wildlife corridors, by the administrative abolition of the shires, and by the growth of aggressive and town-centred local government. Everything – from modern building methods to the heathen culture of the cities – threatens the countryside. And yet the countryside survives, occupying a favourite place in every English person's image of his homeland. Should we wilfully damage the tapestry, by alienating those who have woven and repaired it?

The countryside expresses our two deepest national characteristics: a love of compromise and a genius for institution-building. The English are famous for their eccentricity. But eccentricity is a *social* phenomenon. We are a nation of joiners, who fortify our oddities by clubbing together with people as weird as ourselves. When an activity appeals to us, it transforms itself at once into one of Burke's 'little platoons', with its rules and rights and dignities. Clubs have imprinted their personalities on our fields as assuredly as the farmers and gentry have imprinted theirs. And this is nowhere more clearly seen than in hunting, which has marked our landscape both physically and morally, so as to distinguish it from every other landscape in the world. It is the pulse and the centre, not only of the delicate web of coverts, spinneys, walls and hedgerows by which wildlife travels through the land, but of our mysterious equestrian culture – the culture which forbids us to eat horsemeat, which makes cruelty to horses an offence that cries out to heaven, and which fills our fields and yards with as many old nags as there are decrepit cows in the streets of India.

In a certain measure the English countryside remains a common possession. This fact is reflected in our land laws, which treats ownership as a 'tenure' from the crown. Our landscape is criss-crossed by ancient rights of way, by footpaths, by-ways and

bridlepaths. All ownership of land is minutely quali-
fied. Concessions for angling may be held by one
person, for shooting by another; the right to grow
crops may be ceded to another, and yet another may
possess a right of way, an easement, or the perpetual
benefit of a covenant that 'runs with the land'. New
Britons probably don't understand this. But Old
Englanders, who were taught their national history,
retain an instinctive empathy towards a countryside
shaped by contest and compromise, under the uninterrupted rule over centuries of the English common
law. It does not go against the grain of an English
farmer that he should preserve woods and hedgerows, even when our rulers in Brussels decide to
subsidize their destruction. If he is a hunting farmer
he will preserve them in any case, and he is used to
the idea that his neighbours have legitimate interests
in the land that he farms.

When William Cobbett embarked on his Rural
Rides through England (enjoying as much hunting as
he could along the way) he believed that the flight of
the population to the industrial towns threatened the
very existence of the countryside. The country has
survived, only to be threatened by a massive move in
the opposite direction. People are fleeing the towns,
from which the sense of community has vanished, and
roaming the countryside in search of their souls,
often with scant respect for the communion of
decencies by which souls are made. From the yuppie
commuter to the hunt saboteur, the 'off-comers' are
received as so many alien forms of life – life which has

lost the art of dwelling. And yet people come to the country from the cities as I did, precisely in order to dwell. Unless they respect the customs through which the land becomes our common home, the newcomers will destroy the thing for which they are seeking, bringing to the landscape the very nomadic void that drove them from the city.

The moral objection to hunting is not one that I accept.* However, it is honestly made and deeply felt. It is therefore necessary to respect it, to concede that decent people may wish to enjoy the benefits of country life, without condoning an activity of which they disapprove. Hunting people must behave with more tact and discretion now than they exercised in Grantley Berkeley's day, and for this we should be glad. The odd thing, however, is that so many of those who object to hunting wish also to forbid it. Many people disapprove of ritual slaughter, on account of the suffering involved – and they are probably a majority. But it does not follow that this practice, central to the religious life of Jews and Muslims, should be banned. Some strongly disapprove of the habit of keeping dogs pent up in city dwellings. Others (myself included) are dismayed by the abundance of domestic cats in suburbia, where they have insufficient territory for their comfort, and where they kill vast numbers of our dwindling songbirds. But by what right could we outlaw these

* See Roger Scruton, *Animal Rights and Wrongs*, Demos, London, 2nd Edition, 1998.

practices on which so many people depend for their happiness? Toleration was one of our English virtues; but New Britain seems unwilling to inherit it. Old England disapproved of many things – adultery, illegitimacy, idleness, drunkenness and swearing – but not for a century or more have any of these been crimes. New Britain disapproves of very little, but wishes all its disapprovals to be law.

Even intolerance has degrees, however. Most 'antis' recognize that, if the law permits hunting, so must they. A vestigial respect for procedure is no bad thing, in a world that takes too many decisions too quickly. But in any dispute there are also the religious zealots, to disagree with whom is to offer proof of your depravity. Such people need a cause, and, when human victims are in short supply, animals provide the substitute, with the added advantage that, unlike human victims, they never tell their champions to get lost.

Those 'antis' who reside in the country are usually of the law-abiding kind. One of them always impresses me: a middle-aged man, living alone in a council house, who comes out to confront the hunt in a postman's uniform. He says nothing, does nothing, but merely stands on his doorstep with a haunted, Kafkaesque expression as though making appeal to authorities who have long since failed to respond. My heart goes out to him, and I always wish to stop and explain that hunting is not the vicious thing that he imagines. But he greets my smiles with wide-eyed terror and amazement.

Sometimes too, I am moved by the saboteurs, at least the more embarrassed among them. These are not country residents, but students from Bristol or Birmingham, who come in broken-down vans, armed with hunting horns and placards, to stand whey-faced and wind-tormented in the path of the hunts-man. Their studies in victimology have all but deprived them of words, and their empty slogans and witless sneers make me both ashamed for them and anxious to invite them home for some tutorials. My former colleagues often seem entirely unconcerned by the plight of their students. Young people need nothing so much as wit, allusion and style. They should be studying advocacy and argument; they should be reading poetry, criticism and the authors who have said things clearly and well. Instead, between bouts of pop music and television, they are handed jargon-ridden drivel by out-dated Parisian gurus, impenetrable texts of sociology, the half-articulate leavings of the grievance trade – yes, and Heidegger, who appeals to the post-modern tutor largely because he makes so little sense. It takes courage, none the less, to stand wordless as Schoen-berg's Moses amid your enemies, armed with nothing but a moral idea.

Not all student activists are quite so dumb, of course. One of the more articulate, Neil Kinnock, had risen to become leader of the Labour Party, which he took into the General Election of 1991 with a promise to abolish fox-hunting. By then the commu-nist regimes had collapsed in Europe, the Cold War

was over, and one of the principal motives for voting
Conservative had disappeared. When the election
took place I was in Brno, and on the night of the vote,
the World Service told me that a Labour victory was
certain – opinion polls left no more room for doubt.
Next morning I left early for Bratislava, trying to put
out of mind the bad news from home. I went there to
visit Ján, a friend who had been in prison during the
last months of the communists. Over the years we
had communicated secretly, discussing politics, literature and religion in letters that had to be smuggled
between us; one of Ján's offences had been to publish
an article in *The Salisbury Review*. We were sitting in
his tiny flat, high up in a miserable tower, overlook-
ing muddy wastes and concrete bunkers, his wife and
children squeezed into the corners of a room where
my presence took up what little space remained. The
subjects we discussed had probably never entered the
mind of Mr Kinnock – Heidegger was one of them. I
thought of number 10 Downing Street, with Kinnock's empty bluster sounding in its many rooms.
And the contrast with Ján (who was also Prime
Minister of his country, though living still in this
communist battery farm) made me realize how easy it
would be to lose my loyalty to Old England, when
Mr Kinnock was in charge and England was no
longer Old. Then Ján remembered to tell me what he
had heard in Parliament that morning: the Conservatives had won! He thought my joy was in Mr Major's
victory. In fact it was in Mr Kinnock's defeat. For, in

that contest of mediocrities, only one issue made
sense to me: the future of hunting.

This is not to say that I am an unpolitischer like
Thomas Mann. Far from it. But now that politicians
spend their time legislating over everything that
comes into their heads, it is impossible to take politics
seriously, except as a growing threat to the rest of us.

I stayed for a while in Eastern Europe. I had
discovered that the post-modern economy contains
lucrative oases. For a while I had taken them to be
mirages, traps for the gullible and the over-excited,
or else exclusive preserves for the public-school boys
I had known at Cambridge, who went with their
third-class degrees into some office in the city, there
to eat lunches and grow fat and bald. But no: call
yourself a 'consultant', and you can stop off in the
shade. With a few nicely printed cards and some
plausible introductions, I was actually making
money. I was part of the joke economy of the
information era. I could even give up teaching.
(Which is in any case only consultancy of another
kind.) When I returned to England, I was beginning
to be master of my fate.

Mr Kinnock's defeat led to a new and harder kind
of saboteur. They came our way one Beaufort
Saturday, in a convoy of buses and vans: jeans,
bovver boots, battle fatigues and ski masks; sticks,
truncheons, and whips – snarling boys in undisci-
plined squads, Hell-bent girls in tightly knit coveys,
their black denims and Doc Martens like the uniform
of some mad American sect. At first they stood and

jeered; but when we failed to respond they formed
into battle lines, and marched across the fields,
trampling crops, blowing hunting horns, and wield-
ing their whips at the horses, their sticks and
truncheons at the riders. If they discovered a
horsebox they would smash the windows. Many
followers, children included, were struck in the face
with sticks and stones. One farmer, wholly uncon-
nected with the hunt, was forced to stop in the road,
so that they could smash up his vehicle and beat him
into agreeing with their views.

During the course of the afternoon the police
arrived. A few officers stood in the park, eyeing the
New British proletariat at play with the nonchalance
of connoisseurs. There were less of us now, and the
aggression of our pursuers was increasing. As we
stood by the covert at Allengrove, a black army
advanced from the wood to surround us, a seething
throng of beetles, featureless and sinister in their
balaclava helmets, their sticks waving like antennae,
their eye-holes staring with the hard unshifting gaze
of warring insects. A leader had emerged: he had
exposed his red face, with its scrappy beard and
thick-lipped snarling mouth, and now muscled up to
the foot-followers to taunt them with moronic jibes.
A few farmers had followed in their jeeps and station-
wagons, and these were quickly smashed. A stone
was hurled at the Field Master, who was taken to
hospital with blood pouring from his face. The heroic
army now converged on the terrier-man, surrounded
him, and pulled him to the ground, seizing his spade.

While the crowd kicked at the motionless form of their victim, the leader gleefully wielded the spade, uttering idiot war-cries and egged on by screaming girls.

In Old England the policeman was the friend of the community. He knew the streets and names and faces on his beat, and was first on the scene in all calamities. He went in pursuit of criminals with the eagerness of a hound after a fox; and he would testify proudly in court, confident that the stern-faced magistrate would back him up with a punishment suited to the crime.

In New Britain the policeman is a nomad in a patrol car. Criminals, he has learned, are dangerous and it is best to stay out of their way. Even if you catch them, they will not be punished, since the law is on their side. The only role for the police is to accuse mild-mannered people of motoring offences – a procedure which is safe, agreeable, and beneficial to statistics.

Although I understood these elementary truths, it did seem to me a trifle odd that criminal damage, grievous bodily harm and aggravated assault were being insolently committed under the very eyes of the law. In the circumstances, I concluded, a return to Old England was our historical right. I was riding Bob, the little black cob who was surely descended from the race of war-horses: all muscle, a short strong neck like a leather punch-bag and a bony head that went down between his knees as he galloped. Alone among the Beaufort horses Bob was prepared

for this event. He looked at the waving sticks and
insect faces, and a wave of ancestral war-lust surged
along his arteries. It was just such a horse that God
referred to, when reminding Job of the wonders of
His creation:

> . . . the glory of his nostrils is terrible.
> He paweth in the valley and rejoiceth in his
> strength: he goeth on to meet the armed men.
> He mocketh at fear, and is not affrighted; neither
> turneth he back from the sword.
> The quiver rattleth against him, the glittering
> spear and the shield.
> He swalloweth the ground with fierceness and
> rage: neither believeth he that it is the sound of
> the trumpet.
> He saith among the trumpets, Ha, ha; and he
> smelleth the battle afar off, the thunder of the
> captains, and the shouting.

Bob said among the trumpets and the jeers 'Ha ha!'
And then, snorting, with ears back, head down and
white blaze leading like a banner, he galloped into the
thick of the enemy. Within seconds they had scattered, the terrier-man saving himself, and the beetles
retreating behind a tree-stump, appalled at the
arbitrary violence inflicted on them, and indignantly
invoking the law.

Such scenes are by no means uncommon. Nothing
else in the post-modern world seems to awaken the
old revolutionary fervour – the 'compassionating

zeal' of Rousseau – so much as the defence of animals. To the snarling phalanx behind the tree-stump we were sadistic murderers. In the face of that all-eclipsing fact, nothing could be said that would justify our actions.

If we think of animals in that way, regarding violence against them as a crime, we damage them and us. To care too much for the individual is to threaten the species. Of course there are animals towards which we *assume* a duty of care. But these domestic animals are mirrors of our kindness, privileged and burdened by the superfluity of love.

This was brought home to me by Bob. One summer he had injured a tendon – perhaps by stepping in a rabbit hole. Periodically he was lame from this, and the lameness was getting worse. The time came when he could no longer hunt; nor could he stay in the field, where he would over-eat and become bloated and hobbling. Nor could he be ridden, since, deprived of hunting, he became increasingly curmudgeonly and depressed, shying at every flutter in the hedgerows. He stood all day in the stable, neighing disconsolately, and in frequent pain. I did the decent thing. Bob was fed to the hounds.

To treat a human being as I treated Bob would be murder. But it was right to put him down: a sure proof that, even in the case where we have a duty of care, we must not think of animals as people. Still less should we think in such a way of foxes.

All the same, we love our animal companions and grieve for them, and this is only natural. I recorded

my feelings over Bob in a letter to an American
friend:

Although it is silly to talk or write about horses to
those who have no deep-down love for them, I
think I should say why he was so important to me
– and the fact of your remoteness from the
equestrian world makes it easier. It is not for his
boldness that I loved him, nor for his beauty;
though, when properly exercised, and without the
grass-fed bubble that inflated him, he was as
beautiful as a cob with odd socks could be. Nor did
I especially value his willingness to tackle whatever obstacle stood before him, nor his ability
somehow or other to get over it – though these
are rare and endearing attributes. All those
qualities which could have been mentioned in the
catalogue at a horse auction had no real significance, although he was a star in every respect.
What mattered to me are other things: the look of
docile acceptance with which he greeted me, when
I came to his stable with a view to buying him and
which endured for ever afterwards; the lively
interest that he took in everything that might be
significant to a spirit squeezed into the brain of a
horse; the fact that he did not merely share my
love of hunting but joined with me side by side in
the excitement, taking the lead when he could, but
never showing the slightest aggression towards
horse, man or dog in his elevated sense of
collective joy, and watching, listening, sniffing for

every least sign of whether and where to gallop on. Each field he entered he scanned at once to find the points of exit and if, in the distance, he saw that a horse was jumping, he would smile all over his body and make for the place. Never did he baulk or refuse, since every jump was his decision, made long in advance of any instructions and with a complete mastery of technique that made instructions superfluous. And if at times he was difficult to hold it was only because it was a matter of honour to him to conduct his campaigns himself, offering his saddle as hospitality, but taking his own line to the common goal of victory.

On his last hunt, as I tried in vain to persuade him towards a stone wall which seemed the easiest and safest way into the next field, he suddenly took hold of the bit, put his head down, and galloped towards the hedge which had so much alarmed me. And sure enough he was right – other horses too, ridden by more knowledgeable followers, were bearing down on the little jumpable section which Bob had noticed, and which he flew ahead of them with a Pegasus leap, so gaining precious seconds in his determination to keep up with the action. Always too his ears were pricked, listening out for the huntsman's horn, and always he knew where the hounds were running, however far ahead. And if, in his last years, he rebelled against the miserable life of an indoor school, and refused to obey his rider when taken out for a dreary hack along the road, who could blame him?

His life, with hunting deleted from it, was like the life of Napoleon on St Helena, an exile from his very self, and a fall towards madness.

Grieving is the offshoot of love — love for the individual, under a duty of care. It has no place in the wild, and those who grieve for hunted animals see things wrongly. The screams of a rabbit caught by a weasel move us to pity, even horror. But, unless the rabbit is our loved companion, we must not grieve for him. The moral law does not tell us to save this suffering creature, but rather to consider his death in the context of his life. Is it, on the whole, better for rabbits, that they should live in an environment where they are preyed upon by weasels? Only if such questions come first in our thinking, will we fulfil our duty towards other species, all of which now depend upon us for their survival. If it is true, as I and many others believe, that the fox is better served by hunting than by any other form of cull, and that all rival practices expose him to far more suffering, then it is not just permissible to hunt, but morally right.

Epilogue

Nostalgia is an unhealthy state of mind. But the study, love and emulation of the past are necessary to our self-understanding. All that has gone most wrong in our century has proceeded from a morbid obsession with the future – a belief in 'new dawns', 'revolutionary transformations', and resurrected nations on the march. The past, unlike the future, can be known, understood and adapted to our current uses. When we cast ourselves free from it, we are swept away by outside forces, adrift on the oceanic tide of happening. The future, which we cannot describe, begins to seem inevitable. This surrender to the unknown persists, despite all the crime and destruction that have been wrought in its name. The idea of Europe now occupies the vacuum left by the socialist millennium and the thousand-year Reich. And the balance of nature has been a victim of this newest folly.

In middle life I stumbled across a living limb of Old England. I was astonished to discover how successful our English ways have been in sustaining the balance among species and the harmony between

people. Old England emerged from a process of social
emendation, one part of which I have described in
this book. It was a process of negotiation, compromise, and a constant jostling from below. Left to
itself it would have brought us into the post-modern
world with the minimum of friction, clothing us in
those 'invented traditions' which are none the less
real for being invented. But it has not been left to
itself. Our legislators are herding us into the future,
banning now one thing, now another, in obedience to
waves of emotion which they neither moderate nor
understand. The debate about fox-hunting amply
displays this. So too does the wider debate about the
countryside. As the culture of subsidies spreads like a
fungus over the landscape, both natural and social
ecology are thrown into disarray. If you doubt this,
then you should read *The Killing of the Countryside*, in
which Graham Harvey spells out exactly what the
Common Agricultural Policy has meant for the wild
life and the tame life of our country. New Britain will
contain wild animals; but they will be parasites,
scavengers and vermin – the crows, magpies, rats
and foxes that live from our suburban waste. It will
contain tame life too, but only in the form of pets and
their sedentary protectors.

I am reminded of the great mystery of communism: how could it have come about, at the moment
in history when human beings were demanding
space, freedom, property, and the free exchange of
goods and labour? During my years of wandering
behind the Wall, I would put the question to officials

and dissidents, to head-down scavengers and upright martyrs for the truth. Nobody whatsoever, I discovered, believed in communism – not even those who mouthed the party slogans or arrested those who didn't mouth them when they should.

Nor was there anybody to blame for this. Blame had been chased from the system, and each person was equally involved in it, receiving the standard-issue chains and binding himself in knots that were taught to him as a Young Pioneer. The cause of the catastrophe was nowhere to be discovered. Nobody gave the orders, but everybody received them and everybody passed them on. Nobody had responsibility for what he did, and those who were punished accepted their fate as though they themselves were the authors of it. The freest action was, from another point of view, a further tightening of the chains, and without anyone intending it, every attempt to defy the system merely increased its power. And all this came from and led to nothing.

In my Potemkin career as a consultant I sometimes visit Brussels, to scatter cards around postmodern offices, and admire the meaningless glossy brochures which my fellow consultants produce for other consultants to read. The officials and apparatchiks of the European institutions need to meet ordinary people at expensive receptions with champagne and canapés – for the future, I have learned, however inevitable it may be, nevertheless requires champagne and canapés if it is to dawn successfully.

Now the only people in Brussels, apart from immigrants and bureaucrats, are consultants. So a consultant obtains an inside view of the new apparatchiks.
It is true that they are more open, more wealthy, and
more given to laughter than their communist coun-
terparts. Nevertheless, there is hardly one of them
who has a good word to say about the European
Union, or who does not tell some joke against it, like
the jokes against communism which were the daily
diet of the Czechs and the Poles.

Again I have found myself in a world where orders
are received but not given, where every move against
the system merely serves to reinforce it, and where
nobody can find anything good to say about the
machine of which he is a resigned and obedient cog.
Like communism the new political order is described
not as a decision or a policy, but as an inexorable
process, one that it is fruitless to resist since it has
been ordained by history.

And this is what you see in the architecture of the
new Brussels – architecture which bears an uncanny
resemblance to the prefab modernism of the communist suburb, such as the one where Ján still lives in
Bratislava. Brussels was once a beautiful city. Indeed,
it was beautiful right up to the moment when it lost
its – admittedly *ersatz* – claim to be a national capital
and became, instead, the capital of the post-modern
world. The old Flemish market survives in fragments
– or at least, the more striking façades have been
kept, in obedience to a dwindling local pride in a
dwindling local history, and a dwindling memory of

dwelling. And the nineteenth-century streets around it, with their magnificent vistas and classical terraces, culminating in syncretic churches and Napoleonic monuments, have also remained – at least in outline. But scattered everywhere among them, and littered all around, are office blocks in bronze and sea-green glass, which curve against the street or slice across the alleyways. Whole streets have been demolished to make room for faceless terraces of concrete, with concealed doorways and plate-glass shop-fronts. In every alleyway an old house is being destroyed, or else 'renovated' to contain a glass and concrete interior behind its dead façade. And pressing on the perimeter are the huge shapeless blocks where the Eurocrats spend their days, laughing cynically over the brave new world of directives and subsidies, and nurturing in their hearts the vague but tenacious longing that the whole thing will go up in smoke.

An 'inexorable process' is destroying Brussels, replacing a human habitation which was once the heart of Brabant with a vast complex of offices where nobody lives. The streets are all but deserted, except for the cars and taxis which take the stuffed suits from meeting to meeting and restaurant to restaurant around the city. The churches are hardly visited, and the economic life of the city depends upon the cheap labour of immigrants, whose presence is resented as a symbol of the global disorder which Brussels is imposing on the world. The outline of the city remains, only because Brussels is now the outline of a city, a collection of spaces marked out, owned and exchanged by anonymous corporations in Washington or Tokyo.

Who planned this? Who decided that things should go this way? Who gave the orders and with what authority? There is only one convincing answer: No-one. That is how it is with 'inexorable processes'. However hard you look, you can find nothing and no-one to blame for them. The very thing which you met at the end of every communist corridor, you meet too in the corridors of Brussels — namely, Nothing.

Heidegger once wrote a sentence, no more curious than any other that came from his pen, but the object of constant ridicule in Oxford common rooms: *Das Nichts nichtet* — nothing noths. I admit that this sentence scarcely supplies in sense what it lacks in poetry. Nevertheless it contains a truth. You feel it all around you in Brussels, like a soft, dissolving rain: noth, noth, noth, until nothing remains but Nothing. If you don't believe me now, just wait a few years, and you will. But it would be better to learn the lesson now — better to become aware of the nothingness that is once again growing in the heart of things. For it is our duty to put something in place of nothing, and love in place of denial.

And that has been the theme of this book. The community that I discovered is one of love and affirmation; it is part of the old world, but only because the old world was like that. It is threatened by the new world, but only because we are ceasing to live for each other, ceasing to be answerable for our actions, ceasing, in short, to care.

But let me give the last word to Heidegger, for whom 'care' is the relation to the world that distinguishes you and me. He defines care thus: 'ahead-of-itself-Being-already-in as Being-alongside'. And that, more or less, is what it feels like, jumping hedges on Barney. The being-alongside is mine; the ahead-of-itself-Being-already-in is Barney's. Hunting gives sense to everything – even to Heidegger.